Cooking on a Budget

Food JENNENE PLUMMER
Styling DONNA HAY
Photography WILLIAM MEPPEM

A J.B. Fairfax Press Publication

INTRODUCTION

It is the challenge of every home cook to produce tasty and economical meals for the family. In this book you will find a collection of old favourites as well as some great new ideas that will fit the bill perfectly.

For the budget-conscious one of the greatest difficulties is entertaining so included is an exciting selection of recipes for the thrifty entertainer – these won't break the bank and they don't scream economy food. Ideal for entertaining family and friends or for special family celebrations, you will never worry again about being able to afford to celebrate a special occasion.

EDITORIAL
Food Editor: Rachel Blackmore
Editor: Linda Venturoni
Editorial and Production Assistant: Danielle Thiris
Editorial Coordinator: Margaret Kelly
Recipe Development: Jennene Plummer

Photography: William Meppem
Styling: Donna Hay
Food Stylist's Assistant: Jody Vassallo

DESIGN AND PRODUCTION
Manager: Sheridan Carter
Senior Production Editor: Anna Maguire
Production Editor: Sheridan Packer
Picture Editor: Kirsten Holmes
Layout and Design: Lulu Dougherty
Cover Design: Michele Withers

Published by J.B. Fairfax Press Pty Limited
80-82 McLachlan Avenue
Rushcutters Bay, NSW 2011, Australia
A.C.N. 003 738 430

Formatted by J.B. Fairfax Press Pty Limited
Printed by Toppan Printing Co, Singapore
PRINTED IN SINGAPORE

© J.B. Fairfax Press Pty Limited, 1996
This book is copyright. No part may be reproduced or transmitted without the written permission of the publisher. Enquiries should be made in writing to the publisher.

JBFP 350
Includes Index
ISBN 1 86343 188 8

DISTRIBUTION AND SALES
Australia: J.B. Fairfax Press Pty Limited
Ph: (02) 361 6366 Fax: (02) 360 6262
United Kingdom: J.B. Fairfax Press Limited
Ph: (01933) 40 2330 Fax: (01933) 40 2234

ABOUT THIS BOOK

INGREDIENTS

Unless otherwise stated the following ingredients are used in this book:

Cream   Double, suitable for whipping
Flour   White flour, plain or standard
Sugar   White sugar

WHAT'S IN A TABLESPOON?

AUSTRALIA
1 tablespoon = 20 mL or 4 teaspoons
NEW ZEALAND
1 tablespoon = 15 mL or 3 teaspoons
UNITED KINGDOM
1 tablespoon = 15 mL or 3 teaspoons
The recipes in this book were tested in Australia where a 20 mL tablespoon is standard. The tablespoon in the New Zealand and the United Kingdom sets of measuring spoons is 15 mL. For recipes using baking powder, gelatine, bicarbonate of soda, small quantities of flour and cornflour, simply add another teaspoon for each tablespoon specified.

CANNED FOODS

Can sizes vary between countries and manufacturers. You may find the quantities in this book are slightly different to what is available. Purchase and use the can size nearest to the suggested size in the recipe.

MICROWAVE IT

Where microwave instructions occur in this book, a microwave oven with a 700 watt output has been used. Wattage on domestic microwave ovens varies between 500 and 1000 watts, so it may be necessary to vary cooking times slightly depending on the wattage of your oven.

CONTENTS

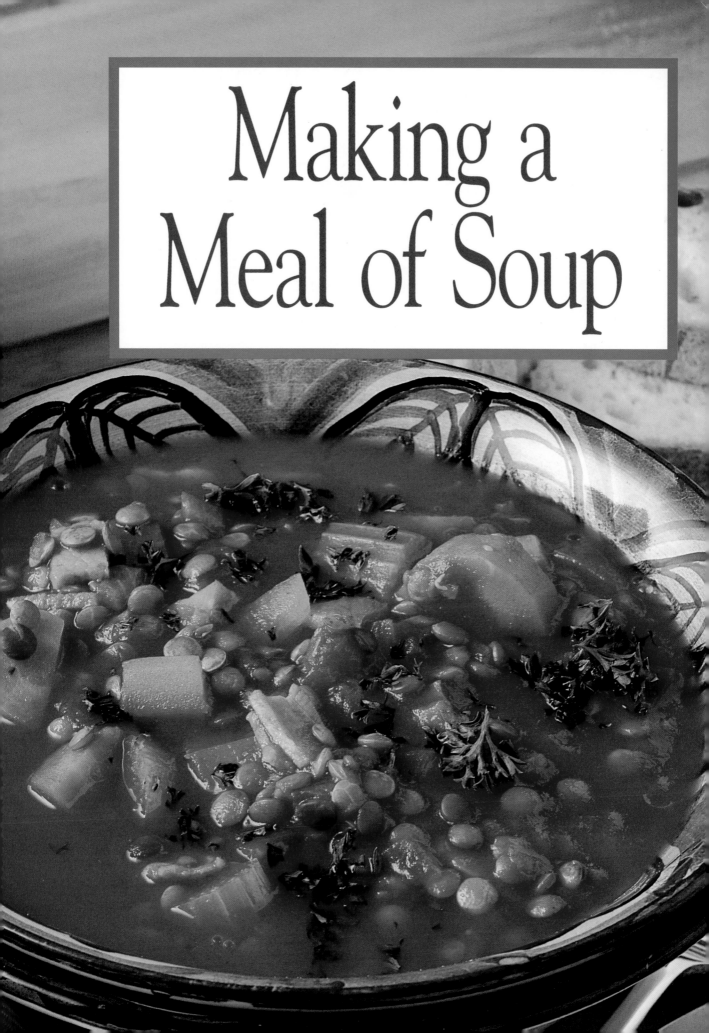

Making a Meal of Soup

ITALIAN MIXED BEAN SOUP

90 g/3 oz dried red kidney beans
90 g/3 oz dried cannellini beans
2 tablespoons olive oil
60 g/2 oz bacon, chopped
1 onion, chopped
1 clove garlic, crushed
3 stalks celery, sliced
2 carrots, chopped
2 potatoes, chopped
6 cups/1.5 litres/2^1/$_2$ pt chicken or
vegetable stock
440 g/14 oz canned tomatoes,
undrained and mashed
^{1}/$_4$ cabbage, finely shredded
60 g/2 oz small pasta shapes or rice
1 teaspoon dried mixed herbs
freshly ground black pepper
grated Parmesan cheese

1 Place red kidney and cannellini beans in a bowl. Cover with cold water and set aside to soak overnight. Drain.

2 Heat oil in a saucepan over a medium heat, add bacon, onion and garlic and cook, stirring, for 5 minutes or until onion is tender. Add celery, carrots and potatoes and cook for 1 minute longer.

3 Stir in stock, tomatoes, cabbage, pasta or rice, red kidney and cannellini beans, herbs and black pepper to taste and bring to the boil. Boil for 10 minutes, then reduce heat and simmer, stirring occasionally, for 1 hour or until beans are tender. Sprinkle with Parmesan cheese and serve.

Serves 4

This minestrone-style soup is delicious served with hot crusty bread.
Extra vegetables of your choice may be added – it is a good way to use up odds and ends of vegetables.

LENTIL AND TOMATO SOUP

250 g/8 oz green, red or brown lentils
440 g /14 oz canned tomatoes,
undrained and mashed
125 g/4 oz bacon, chopped
3 stalks celery, chopped
2 onions, chopped
2 carrots, chopped
1 clove garlic, crushed
1 bay leaf
^{1}/$_2$ teaspoon dried mixed herbs
2 tablespoons tomato paste (purée)
4 cups/1 litre/1^3/$_4$ pt chicken or
vegetable stock
freshly ground black pepper
chopped fresh parsley

Place lentils, tomatoes, bacon, celery, onions, carrots, garlic, bay leaf, herbs, tomato paste (purée), stock and black pepper to taste in a large saucepan. Bring to the boil, then reduce heat, cover and simmer, stirring occasionally, for 1 hour or until lentils are tender. Sprinkle with parsley and serve.

Serves 4

Serve with crusty bread, soda bread, savoury scones or homemade damper, see recipe page 80. Any colour lentils can be used to make soups – just choose the cheapest.

Hearty Vegetable Soup

Hearty Vegetable Soup

500 g/1 lb lamb, such as neck chops
or 2 lamb shanks (knuckles)
8 cups/2 litres/3^1/$_2$ pt water
4 stalks celery, chopped
3 carrots, chopped
2 onions, chopped
1 turnip, chopped
90 g/3 oz soup mix or barley
1 teaspoon dried mixed herbs
freshly ground black pepper

1   Place lamb, water, celery, carrots, onions, turnip, soup mix or barley, herbs and black pepper to taste in a saucepan. Bring to the boil, then reduce heat, cover and simmer, stirring occasionally, for 1 hour or until all ingredients are tender.

2   Remove lamb from soup and cool slightly. Remove meat from bones and return to soup. Discard bones. Bring soup to the boil over a medium heat and simmer, stirring, for 2-3 minutes or until heated through.

Serves 4

For a change use 125 g/ 4 oz chopped beef stewing steak in place of the lamb. Whatever meat you choose for this soup select a low-cost stewing cut. Soup mix is a mixture of dried peas and barley available in the pulses section of your supermarket.

MIXED SEAFOOD SOUP

6 cups/1.5 litres/2$\frac{1}{2}$ pt water
500 g/1 lb boneless fish fillets
1 onion, roughly chopped
1 stalk celery, chopped
1 teaspoon black peppercorns
440 g/14 oz canned tomatoes,
undrained and mashed
1 potato, chopped
1 tablespoon tomato paste (purée)
1 clove garlic, crushed
1 teaspoon dried oregano
freshly ground black pepper
250 g/8 oz mussels, scrubbed and
beards removed
125 g/4 oz squid (calamari) rings
2 tablespoons chopped fresh parsley

A little chopped fresh red chilli or chilli sauce adds a delicious bite to this soup. When the budget is very tight it is just as tasty made with fish fillets only.

Serves 4

1   Place water, fish, onion, celery and black peppercorns in a saucepan and slowly bring to the boil over a medium heat. Reduce heat, cover and simmer for 15 minutes. Strain liquid. Flake fish and reserve. Discard vegetables.

2   Return stock to a clean saucepan, add tomatoes, potato, tomato paste (purée), garlic, oregano and black pepper to taste and bring to the boil. Reduce heat and simmer for 30 minutes.

3   Add mussels, cover and cook for 5 minutes or until shells open. Discard any mussels that do not open after 5 minutes cooking. Add squid (calamari) and reserved fish and simmer for 2-3 minutes or until soup is hot. Sprinkle with parsley and serve.

SMOKED FISH CHOWDER

30 g/1 oz butter
1 onion, chopped
1 clove garlic, crushed
2 potatoes, chopped
$\frac{1}{4}$ cup/30 g/1 oz flour
2 cups/500 mL/16 fl oz milk
2 cups/500 mL/16 fl oz water
500 g/1 lb smoked cod or haddock,
skinned, boned and cut into chunks
2 zucchini (courgettes), chopped
3 spring onions, chopped
freshly ground black pepper
3 tablespoons chopped fresh parsley
2 teaspoons chopped fresh dill

A chowder is a thickened soup usually of seafood and vegetables. The word itself is a corruption of the French name for a huge copper vessel known as a chaudière in which communal meals were prepared. If the budget permits, add other seafood such as mussel meat, canned crab or prawns.

Serves 4

1   Melt butter in a saucepan over a medium heat, add onion and garlic and cook, stirring, for 5 minutes or until onion is tender. Add potatoes and cook, stirring, for 1 minute.

2   Blend flour with a little of the milk to make a smooth paste and stir into potato mixture. Add remaining milk and water to pan and bring to the boil. Cook, stirring constantly, for 5-8 minutes or until mixture thickens. Reduce heat and simmer for 15 minutes or until potatoes are tender.

3   Add fish, zucchini (courgettes), spring onions and black pepper to taste and simmer for 10 minutes or until fish is tender. Stir in parsley and dill and serve immediately.

MULLIGATAWNY SOUP

1 tablespoon vegetable oil
2 onions, chopped
1 green apple, cored, peeled and
chopped
1 clove garlic, crushed
2 tablespoons lemon juice
1 tablespoon curry powder
1 teaspoon brown sugar
$^1/_2$ teaspoon ground cumin
$^1/_4$ teaspoon ground coriander
2 tablespoons flour
8 cups/2 litres/3$^1/_2$ pt chicken stock
500 g/1 lb boneless chicken breast or
thigh fillets, cut into 1 cm/$^1/_2$ in cubes
$^1/_3$ cup/75 g/2$^1/_2$ oz rice
freshly ground black pepper

1   Heat oil in a large saucepan over a medium heat, add onions, apple and garlic and cook, stirring, for 5 minutes or until onions are tender. Add lemon juice, curry powder, sugar, cumin and coriander and cook over a low heat, stirring, for 10 minutes or until fragrant.

2   Blend flour with a little stock and stir into curry mixture. Add chicken, rice and remaining stock to pan and stirring constantly, bring to the boil. Reduce heat, cover and simmer for 20 minutes or until chicken and rice are cooked. Season to taste with black pepper.

Serves 4

A dash of chilli sauce and a chopped tomato are delicious additions to this soup. Serve with crusty bread rolls, naan or pitta bread.

Plate and soup bowl/Villeroy & Boch

SPICY LAKSA

Left: Mulligatawny Soup
Above: Spicy Laksa

4 cups/1 litre/1³/4 pt chicken stock
4 chicken thigh fillets or
2 boneless chicken breast fillets
1 tablespoon vegetable oil
1 onion, chopped
1 clove garlic, crushed
1 teaspoon chopped fresh red chilli
1 teaspoon ground coriander
1 teaspoon ground turmeric
2 cups/500 mL/16 fl oz milk
1 cup/250 mL/8 fl oz coconut milk
250 g/8 oz rice noodles, soaked
and drained
125 g/4 oz bean sprouts

1   Place stock in a saucepan and bring to the boil over a medium heat. Add chicken, then reduce heat, cover and simmer for 5 minutes. Using a slotted spoon, remove chicken from liquid and set aside. Transfer liquid to a bowl.

2   Heat oil in the same pan over a medium heat, add onion, garlic, chilli, coriander and turmeric and cook, stirring, for 5 minutes or until onion is tender. Return liquid to pan and stir in milk and coconut milk. Bring to the boil, then reduce heat and simmer, stirring constantly, for 10 minutes.

3   Cut chicken into thick strips. Add chicken, noodles and bean sprouts to soup and bring to simmering over a medium heat. Simmer, stirring occasionally, for 5 minutes or until chicken is heated through and tender.

Serves 6

Rice noodles, also called rice vermicelli or rice sticks, vary in size from a narrow vermicelli style to a ribbon noodle about 5 mm/¹/4 in wide. They should be soaked before using; the narrow noodles require about 10 minutes soaking, while the wider ones will need about 30 minutes.

13

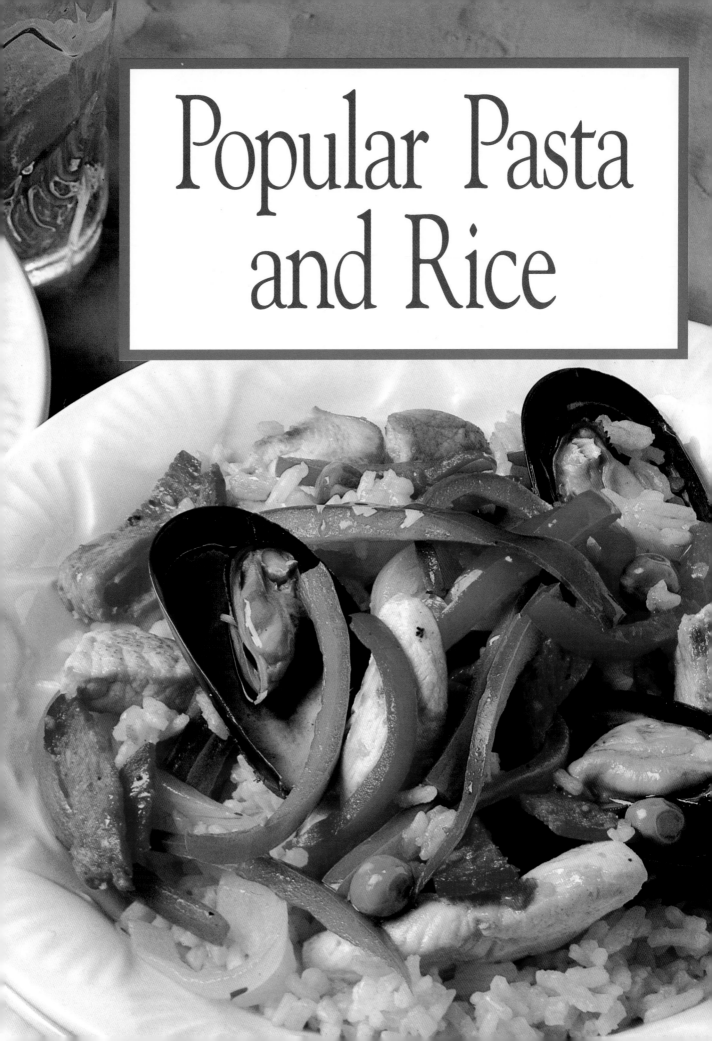

Popular Pasta
and Rice

FAMILY PAELLA

¹/₄ cup/60 mL/2 fl oz olive oil
4 chicken thigh fillets or 2 boneless
chicken breast fillets, sliced
250 g/8 oz diced lean pork
2 onions, chopped
1 small red or green pepper, sliced
60 g/2 oz hot Spanish salami, sliced
3 cups/660 g/1 lb 5 oz rice
3 cups/750 mL/1¹/₄ pt chicken stock
or water
¹/₂ teaspoon ground turmeric
freshly ground black pepper
500 g/1 lb mussels, scrubbed and
beards removed
60 g/2 oz frozen peas

For a complete meal serve
with crusty bread and a
tossed green salad.
If the budget permits, add
a few uncooked prawns
and sliced squid (calamari)
in step 4 with a squeeze of
lemon juice for flavour. A
combination of water or
stock and white wine may
be used as the cooking
liquid.

1 Heat oil in a large frying pan over a
medium heat, add chicken and pork
and cook, stirring, for 3 minutes. Using
a slotted spoon, remove from pan and
set aside.

2 Add onions, red or green pepper
and salami to pan and cook, stirring,
for 5 minutes or until onions are
tender. Add rice and cook, stirring,
for 1 minute or until rice is coated
with oil.

3 Stir stock or water, turmeric and
black pepper to taste into pan and
bring to the boil. Reduce heat and
simmer for 5 minutes. Add mussels and
peas, cover and simmer for 5 minutes
or until mussels open. Discard any
mussels that do not open after
5 minutes cooking.

4 Return chicken and pork to pan and
simmer, uncovered, for 5-10 minutes or
until all the liquid is absorbed and rice
is tender. Serve immediately.

Serves 6

KEDGEREE

60 g/2 oz butter
2 onions, chopped
1 small red or green pepper, chopped
2 teaspoons cornflour blended with
1 cup/250 mL/8 fl oz milk
500 g/1 lb smoked cod or haddock,
boned, skinned and chopped
125 g/4 oz frozen peas
125 g/4 oz canned sweet corn kernels,
drained
2 cups/440 g/14 oz rice, cooked
2 tablespoons lemon juice
freshly ground black pepper
2 hard-boiled eggs, chopped
2 tablespoons chopped fresh parsley

When avocados are in
season, stir in a chopped
avocado with the rice in
step 3. Serve Kedgeree with
toasted French bread.

1 Melt butter in a frying pan over a
medium heat, add onions and red or
green pepper and cook, stirring, for
5 minutes or until onion is tender.

2 Remove pan from heat and stir in
milk mixture. Return pan to heat and
stirring constantly, bring to the boil.
Add fish, peas and sweet corn, reduce
heat and simmer for 5 minutes or until
fish flakes when test with a fork.

3 Stir rice, lemon juice and black
pepper to taste into pan and simmer,
stirring occasionally, for 5 minutes or
until mixture is heated. Top with eggs
and sprinkle with parsley.

Serves 6

VEGETABLE AND TUNA RISOTTO

2 tablespoons olive oil
1 onion, chopped
1 clove garlic, crushed
60 g/2 oz button mushrooms, chopped
1 zucchini (courgette), chopped
1 tomato, chopped
$^1/_2$ red or green pepper, chopped
2 cups/440 g/14 oz arborio or
risotto rice
5 cups/1.2 litres/2 pt hot
chicken stock
2 tablespoons lemon juice
60 g/2 oz frozen peas
220 g/7 oz canned tuna, drained
and flaked
freshly ground black pepper
grated Parmesan cheese

1 Heat oil in a frying pan over a medium heat, add onion and garlic and cook, stirring, for 4-5 minutes or until onion is tender. Add mushrooms, zucchini (courgette), tomato and red or green pepper and cook, stirring, for 2 minutes.

2 Add rice to pan and stir well to coat with oil. Pour 1 cup/250 mL/8 fl oz stock into rice mixture and cook, stirring constantly, until stock is absorbed. Add another 1 cup/250 mL/ 8 fl oz stock and continue cooking as described until all but 1 cup/250 mL/ 8 fl oz stock is used. Add lemon juice, peas and remaining stock and cook, until rice is tender, peas are cooked and stock is absorbed.

3 Add tuna and black pepper to taste and heat, stirring gently, for 2-3 minutes or until tuna is hot. Sprinkle with Parmesan cheese.

Serves 4

To make chicken stock, place cooked or raw chicken bones or carcass and roughly chopped onion, carrot and celery in a saucepan. Cover with cold water. Add black peppercorns and a sprig of parsley. Bring to the boil, then cover and simmer for 1 hour. Strain stock, discard vegetables, cool and use as desired or freeze.

Kedgeree

ALMOND LAMB PILAU

2 tablespoons olive oil
1 onion, chopped
1 clove garlic, crushed
500 g/1 lb diced lamb
2 teaspoons curry powder
2 teaspoons ground coriander
1 teaspoon ground cumin
1 teaspoon ground ginger
$^1/_2$ teaspoon ground turmeric
$2^1/_2$ cups/600 mL/1 pt chicken stock
1 tomato, chopped
freshly ground black pepper
2 cups/440 g/14 oz rice
90 g/3 oz almonds, toasted
90 g/3 oz raisins

Accompany pilau with a tossed green salad or steamed green vegetables or your choice, natural yogurt and a selection of traditional Indian accompaniments, such as pappadums, mango chutney and sambals.

1 Heat oil in a frying pan over a medium heat, add onion and garlic and cook, stirring, for 5 minutes or until onion is tender. Add lamb and cook, stirring occasionally, for 5 minutes or until lamb is brown on all sides.

2 Add curry powder, coriander, cumin, ginger and turmeric to pan and cook, stirring constantly, for 2 minutes or until fragrant. Add $^1/_2$ cup/125 mL/ 4 fl oz stock, tomato and black pepper to taste and bring to the boil. Reduce heat, cover and simmer, stirring occasionally, for 20 minutes or until lamb is tender.

3 Add remaining stock to pan and bring to the boil. Stir in rice, reduce heat, cover and simmer for 15 minutes or until rice is cooked. Add almonds and raisins and using a fork toss to combine.

Serves 6

18

RICE AND PASTA SALAD

Left: Almond Lamb Pilau
Above: Rice and Pasta Salad

125 g/4 oz small pasta of your choice
1 cup/220 g/7 oz rice, cooked
440 g/14 oz canned tuna, drained and
flaked
315 g/10 oz canned sweet corn
kernels, drained
2 tomatoes, chopped
2 stalks celery, chopped
1 onion, sliced
1 small red or green pepper, chopped
1 small cucumber, sliced
lettuce leaves of your choice

ORANGE AND MUSTARD
DRESSING
$^1/_4$ cup/60 mL/2 fl oz olive oil
1 tablespoon orange juice
1 tablespoon vinegar
$^1/_2$ teaspoon mild mustard
freshly ground black pepper

1   Cook pasta in boiling water in
a large saucepan following packet
directions. Drain, rinse under cold
running water and set aside to cool.

2   Place pasta, rice, tuna, sweet corn,
tomatoes, celery, onion, red or green
pepper and cucumber in a large bowl
and toss to combine.

3   To make dressing, place oil, orange
juice, vinegar, mustard and black
pepper to taste in a screwtop jar and
shake well to combine. Spoon dressing
over salad and toss. Line a serving
platter with lettuce leaves, top with
pasta mixture and serve.

Serves 6

For something different
serve salad in pitta bread
pockets lined with lettuce
leaves.

VEGETABLE AND BEAN LASAGNE

Oven temperature
180°C, 350°F, Gas 4

250 g/8 oz instant (no precooking required) lasagne

MUSTARD CHEESE SAUCE
90 g/3 oz butter
$^1/_3$ cup/45 g/1$^1/_2$ oz flour
3 cups/750 mL/1$^1/_4$ pt milk
125 g/4 oz grated tasty cheese
(mature Cheddar)
$^1/_4$ teaspoon dry mustard
freshly ground black pepper

BEAN AND VEGETABLE SAUCE
1 tablespoon olive oil
1 onion, chopped
1 clove garlic, crushed
2 stalks celery, chopped
2 carrots, chopped
1 zucchini (courgette), sliced
1 small red or green pepper, chopped
125 g/4 oz frozen green beans
440 g/14 oz canned tomatoes,
undrained and mashed
315 g/10 oz canned red kidney beans,
drained and rinsed
$^1/_2$ cup/125 mL/4 fl oz red wine or
water
$^1/_2$ teaspoon dried basil or
oregano leaves

CREAM CHEESE TOPPING
$^1/_2$ cup/125 mL/4 fl oz cream (double)
60 g/2 oz grated tasty cheese
(mature Cheddar)
2 tablespoons grated Parmesan cheese

1 To make cheese sauce, melt butter in a saucepan over a medium heat, stir in flour and cook for 1 minute. Remove pan from heat and gradually whisk in milk. Return pan to heat and cook, stirring constantly, for 6-8 minutes or until sauce boils and thickens. Reduce heat and simmer for 3 minutes. Remove pan from heat, stir in tasty cheese (mature Cheddar), mustard and black pepper to taste. Set aside to cool.

2 To make vegetable sauce, heat oil in a large frying pan over a medium heat, add onion and garlic and cook, stirring, for 5 minutes or until onion is tender. Add celery, carrots, zucchini (courgette), red or green pepper and green beans and cook, stirring, for 1 minute. Stir in tomatoes, red kidney beans, wine or water and basil or oregano and bring to the boil. Reduce heat and simmer for 15 minutes. Remove pan from heat and set aside to cool.

3 Spread half the vegetable sauce over the base of an ovenproof dish. Top with half the cheese sauce and cover with lasagne sheets, breaking them to fit if necessary. Repeat layers to use remaining ingredients.

4 For topping, pour cream evenly over lasagne, then sprinkle with tasty cheese (mature Cheddar) and Parmesan cheese and bake for 30-35 minutes or until topping is golden and mixture bubbling.

Serves 6

Any pasta can be used in place of the lasagne if you wish. Use 500 g/1 lb cooked pasta of your choice and layer as described in recipe.

Spinach and Ricotta Cannelloni

SPINACH AND RICOTTA CANNELLONI

250 g/8 oz instant (no precooking
required) cannelloni tubes
440 g/14 oz canned tomatoes, drained
and chopped
1 clove garlic, crushed
125 g/4 oz grated mozzarella cheese
2 tablespoons grated Parmesan cheese

SPINACH FILLING
$^1/_2$ bunch/250 g/8 oz English spinach,
shredded
$^1/_2$ cup/125 mL/4 fl oz water
250 g/8 oz ricotta cheese, drained
2 tablespoons grated Parmesan cheese
1 egg, beaten
$^1/_4$ teaspoon ground nutmeg
freshly ground black pepper

Serves 4

1 To make filling, place spinach and water in a saucepan, cover with a tight fitting lid and cook over a medium heat, shaking pan occasionally, for 4-5 minutes or until spinach wilts. Drain well, squeezing out excess water and set aside to cool.

2 Finely chop spinach and place in a bowl. Add ricotta cheese, Parmesan cheese, egg, nutmeg and black pepper to taste and mix to combine. Spoon mixture into cannelloni tubes and arrange tubes side-by-side in a lightly greased ovenproof dish.

3 Combine tomatoes and garlic in a bowl and spoon over cannelloni. Sprinkle with mozzarella cheese and Parmesan cheese and bake for 30-35 minutes or until cannelloni is tender and top is golden.

Oven temperature
180°C, 350°F, Gas 4

Cottage cheese may be used in place of the ricotta cheese if you wish. If using cottage cheese, push through a sieve to achieve a smoother texture. Serve cannelloni with an Italian salad and herb or garlic bread.

CREAMY MUSHROOM GNOCCHI

Oven temperature
180°C, 350°F, Gas 4

500 g/1 lb potatoes, cooked
2 cups/250 g/8 oz flour, sifted
30 g/1 oz butter, melted
30 g/1 oz grated Parmesan cheese
freshly ground black pepper

MUSHROOM SAUCE
30 g/1 oz butter
125 g/4 oz button mushrooms, sliced
2 tablespoons wholegrain mustard
1 cup/250 mL/8 fl oz cream (double)
60 g/2 oz grated tasty cheese
(mature Cheddar)
30 g/1 oz grated Parmesan cheese

1   Place potatoes in a bowl and mash. Add flour, butter, half the Parmesan cheese and black pepper to taste and mix to make a stiff dough. Turn dough onto a lightly floured surface and knead until smooth. Shape dough into 2.5 cm/1 in ovals and press with the back of a fork.

2   Cook gnocchi, in batches, in boiling water in a large saucepan for 3 minutes or until they rise to the surface. Using a slotted spoon, remove gnocchi from pan and place in a greased shallow, ovenproof dish.

3   To make sauce, melt butter in a frying pan over a medium heat, add mushrooms and cook, stirring, for 5 minutes. Stir in mustard and cream and bring to the boil, reduce heat and simmer for 10 minutes or until sauce reduces and thickens.

4   Spoon sauce over gnocchi. Sprinkle with tasty cheese (mature Cheddar) and Parmesan cheese and bake for 10-15 minutes or until cheese melts.

Serves 4

For a delicious alternative, shred 250 g/8 oz English spinach and blanch in boiling water for 1 minute. Drain well and squeeze to remove as much liquid as possible, then stir into potato mixture. Serve gnocchi with crusty bread and a salad of crisp vegetables and mixed lettuces.

PENNE WITH PEPERONI SAUCE

500 g/1 lb penne

PEPERONI SAUCE
1 tablespoon olive oil
1 onion, sliced
1 clove garlic, crushed
1 baby eggplant (aubergine), sliced
60 g/2 oz peperoni, sliced
440 g/14 oz canned tomato purée
(passata)
$^1/_2$ cup/125 mL/4 fl oz red wine or water
60 g/2 oz frozen peas
freshly ground black pepper

1   To make sauce, heat oil in a frying pan over a medium heat, add onion and garlic and cook, stirring, for 2-3 minutes or until onion is soft. Add eggplant (aubergine) and peperoni and cook, stirring, for 2 minutes.

2   Stir tomato purée (passata) and wine or water into pan and bring to the boil. Reduce heat and simmer, stirring occasionally, for 15 minutes or until sauce reduces and thickens. Add peas and simmer for 5 minutes longer or until peas are cooked. Season to taste with black pepper.

3   Cook pasta in boiling water in a large saucepan following packet directions. Drain, place in a serving bowl, spoon over sauce and serve immediately.

For something different sliced fresh mushrooms and a dash of chilli sauce can be added to the Peperoni Sauce.

Serves 4

Bean and Lentil Feasts

*Previous pages: Spicy Sausage
Hot Pot, Garlic and Almond Beans*
Bowl Royal Worcester, *Plate* Villeroy & Boch

SPICY SAUSAGE HOT POT

315 g/10 oz lentils
1 tablespoon olive oil
2 spicy Polish sausages, sliced
1 onion, chopped
1 clove garlic, crushed
2 tablespoons curry powder
2 teaspoons ground coriander
1 teaspoon ground ginger
1 teaspoon ground cumin
1 carrot, chopped
250 g/8 oz cauliflower, broken into
small florets
440 g/14 oz canned tomatoes, drained
and chopped
$^1/_2$ cup/125 mL/4 fl oz chicken stock
2 tablespoons lemon juice
freshly ground black pepper
$^1/_2$ small cabbage, shredded

1   Place lentils in a saucepan, pour over enough cold water to cover and bring to the boil over a medium heat. Reduce heat and simmer for 15-20 minutes or until lentils are cooked. Drain and set aside.

2   Heat oil in frying pan, over a medium heat, add sausages and cook for 2-3 minutes. Remove sausages and set aside.

3   Add onion and garlic to pan and cook, stirring, for 3-4 minutes or until onion is tender. Stir in curry powder, coriander, ginger and cumin and cook, stirring, for 2 minutes or until fragrant.

4   Add cooked lentils, sausages, carrot, cauliflower, tomatoes, stock, lemon juice and black pepper to taste and bring to the boil, reduce heat and simmer, stirring occasionally, for 5 minutes or until vegetables are tender. Add cabbage and cook for 3-5 minutes longer or until cabbage just wilts. Serve immediately.

Serves 4

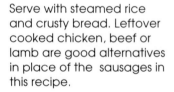

Serve with steamed rice and crusty bread. Leftover cooked chicken, beef or lamb are good alternatives in place of the sausages in this recipe.

GARLIC AND ALMOND BEANS

2 tablespoons olive oil
1 small red onion, sliced
30 g/1 oz flaked almonds
3 cloves garlic, crushed
125 g/4 oz green beans, sliced
1 red pepper, chopped
60 g/2 oz snow peas (mangetout)
1 red chilli, chopped
freshly ground black pepper

1   Heat oil in a frying pan cook over a medium heat, add onion, almonds and garlic and cook, stirring, for 5 minutes or until almonds are golden.

2   Add green beans, red pepper, snow peas (mangetout) and chilli and cook, stirring, for 2 minutes or until heated through. Season to taste with black pepper.

Serves 6

This dish makes an interesting accompaniment to grilled or pan cooked meat or chicken.

BEAN HUNZA PIE

1 cup/125 g/4 oz flour
1 cup/155 g/5 oz wholemeal flour
125 g/4 oz butter, chopped
^{1}/3 cup/90 mL/3 fl oz water
milk

BEAN AND VEGETABLE FILLING
125 g/4 oz dried red kidney beans,
soaked overnight and drained
4 potatoes, cubed and cooked
^{1}/2 bunch/250 g/8 oz English spinach,
chopped and blanched
250 g/8 oz cottage cheese
2 tomatoes, chopped
1 onion, chopped
2 tablespoons tomato paste (purée)
1 teaspoon dried mixed herbs
^{1}/2 teaspoon cayenne pepper
^{1}/4 teaspoon ground nutmeg
freshly ground black pepper

1 To make filling, place red kidney beans in a saucepan, cover with cold water and bring the boil. Boil for 10 minutes, reduce heat and simmer for 1 hour or until beans are tender. Drain and set aside to cool.

2 Place beans, potatoes, spinach, cottage cheese, tomatoes, onion, tomato paste (purée), herbs, cayenne pepper, nutmeg and black pepper to taste in a bowl and mix to combine. Set aside.

3 Place flour and wholemeal flour in a bowl and mix to combine. Rub in butter with fingertips until mixture resembles fine breadcrumbs. Mix in enough water to make a pliable dough. Wrap dough in plastic food wrap and refrigerate for 20 minutes.

4 Roll out half the dough to 3 mm/^{1}/8 in thick, cut out a 23 cm/9 in circle and place on a lightly greased baking tray. Spoon filling onto pastry leaving a 2 cm/^{3}/4 in border. Brush border with milk.

5 Roll out remaining pastry and cut out a 30 cm/12 in circle. Place pastry circle over filling and press edges together to seal. Trim and decorate edges and brush top of pie with milk. Cut a steam vent in top of pie and bake for 30-35 minutes or until pastry is golden. Serve hot, warm or cold.

Serves 6

Oven temperature
200°C, 400°F, Gas 6

To blanch spinach, plunge it into boiling water for 30-60 seconds. Drain and refresh under cold running water to stop the cooking process. Drain again, ensuring excess water is removed by pressing spinach between two plates. A little grated tasty cheese (mature Cheddar) may be added to the filling.

Bean Hunza Pie

Plate Waterford Wedgwood

CRUNCHY CHICKPEA SALAD

185 g/6 oz dried chickpeas, soaked
overnight and drained
$^1/4$ cup/60 mL/2 fl oz olive oil
2 cloves garlic, crushed
2 teaspoons curry powder
1 teaspoon ground cumin
2 potatoes, cubed
2 baby eggplant (aubergines), sliced
2 tomatoes, chopped
1 bunch/500 g/1 lb English spinach

LEMON AND CHILLI DRESSING
$^1/4$ cup/60 mL/2 fl oz olive oil
2 tablespoons lemon juice
1 clove garlic, crushed
1 teaspoon chopped fresh red chilli
$^1/2$ teaspoon ground coriander

1 Place chickpeas in a saucepan, cover with cold water and bring the boil. Boil for 10 minutes, then reduce heat and simmer for 30-40 minutes or until chickpeas are just tender. Drain well and set aside.

2 Heat 2 tablespoons oil in a frying pan over a medium heat, add garlic, curry powder and cumin and cook, stirring, for 1 minute or until fragrant. Add chickpeas and cook, stirring, for 3-5 minutes or until golden. Using a slotted spoon, remove chickpeas and place a large bowl.

3 Add potatoes to frying pan and cook, stirring constantly, for 8-10 minutes or until potatoes are cooked and golden. Remove from pan and add to chickpeas.

4 Brush eggplant (aubergines) with remaining oil and cook under a preheated medium grill or 4-5 minutes each side or until golden and tender. Add eggplant (aubergines) and tomatoes to chickpea mixture and toss to combine.

5 Line a large serving platter with spinach leaves and pile chickpea mixture in the centre.

6 To make dressing, place oil, lemon juice, garlic, chilli and coriander in a screwtop jar and shake well to combine. Drizzle dressing over salad.

Serves 6

This salad may be served at room temperature or chilled.

Crunchy Chickpea Salad

BEANS WITH TOMATO AND TUNA

375 g/12 oz dried cannellini beans,
soaked overnight and drained
2 tablespoons olive oil
1 onion, sliced
1 stalk celery, sliced
1 clove garlic, crushed
440 g/14 oz canned tomatoes,
undrained and mashed
$^1/_2$ cup/125 mL/4 fl oz water
$^1/_2$ teaspoon dried basil
$^1/_4$ teaspoon dried sage
$^1/_4$ teaspoon sugar
freshly ground black pepper
220 g/7 oz canned tuna, drained and
flaked (optional)

Served hot or cold, these beans are delicious as part of an antipasto platter or as a salad on a bed of lettuce. Toss through a few sliced artichoke hearts for a change when the budget allows. Another time, omit the tuna and serve as a side dish for grilled meats or as part of a vegetarian meal.

1 Place cannellini beans in a saucepan, cover with cold water and bring to the boil. Boil for 10 minutes, then reduce heat and simmer for 1 hour or until beans are tender. Drain and set aside.

2 Heat oil in a frying pan over a medium heat, add onion, celery and garlic and cook, stirring, for 5 minutes or until onion is tender. Add beans, tomatoes, water, basil, sage, sugar and black pepper to taste and bring to the boil. Reduce heat and simmer, stirring occasionally, for 30 minutes. Stir in tuna, if using, and simmer for 5 minutes longer or until heated through.

Serves 4

Bean Enchiladas

12 flour tortillas
60 g/2 oz grated tasty cheese
(mature Cheddar) (optional)

BEAN AND CORN FILLING
375 g/12 oz dried red kidney beans
125 g/4 oz canned creamed sweet corn
2 tablespoons sour cream

TOMATO AND OLIVE SALSA
4 tomatoes, chopped
2 tablespoons chopped stuffed green
olives (optional)
2 tablespoons chopped fresh coriander
freshly ground black pepper

1 To make filling, place red kidney beans in a bowl. Cover with cold water and set aside to soak overnight. Drain.

2 Place red kidney beans in a saucepan, cover with cold water and bring the boil. Boil for 10 minutes, then reduce heat and simmer for 1 hour or until beans are tender. Drain and place in a bowl. Add sweet corn and sour cream and mix to combine.

3 Spoon filling down the centre of each tortilla and roll up. Arrange rolls side-by-side in a lightly greased ovenproof dish, sprinkle with cheese, if using, and bake for 20-25 minutes.

4 To make salsa, place tomatoes, olives, if using, coriander and black pepper to taste in a bowl and toss to combine.

5 To serve, arrange rolls on serving plates and spoon over salsa.

Serves 6

Oven temperature
180°C, 350°F, Gas 4

This filling mixture can also be used as a filling for tacos or a topping for nachos. Garnish tacos or nachos with mashed avocado, sour cream and grated tasty cheese (mature Cheddar).

Left: Beans with Tomato and Tuna
Right: Bean Enchiladas

Lentil and Spinach Quiche

Oven temperature
200°C, 400°F, Gas 6

The pastry used in Bean Hunza Pie can be used for this quiche.

250 g/8 oz prepared wholemeal pastry
2 tablespoons sesame seeds, toasted

LENTIL AND SPINACH FILLING
200 g/6^1/2 oz lentils
2 tablespoons olive oil
1 onion, chopped
2 cloves garlic, crushed
60 g/2 oz button mushrooms, sliced
2 teaspoons chilli powder
1 teaspoon ground ginger
1 bunch/500 g/1 lb English spinach, chopped
3 tomatoes, peeled and chopped
2 tablespoons lemon juice
200 g/6^1/2 oz ricotta cheese, drained
1 egg, lightly beaten
freshly ground black pepper

1 Roll out pastry to 5 mm/^{1}/4 in thick and use to line a greased 25 cm/10 in flan tin. Prick base and sides of pastry with a fork, line with nonstick baking paper and fill with uncooked rice. Bake for 10-15 minutes or until lightly browned, them remove rice and paper and set aside to cool.

2 To make filling, place lentils in a saucepan, cover with cold water and bring to the boil. Reduce heat and simmer for 15-20 minutes or until lentils are cooked. Drain and set aside.

3 Heat oil in a large frying pan over a medium heat, add onion and garlic and cook, stirring for 3-4 minutes or until onion is soft. Add mushrooms and cook for 2 minutes. Add chilli powder and ginger and cook for 1 minute.

4 Add spinach to pan, cover and cook for 2 minutes or until spinach just wilts. Drain off any excess moisture, then stir in lentils, tomatoes and lemon juice. Set aside to cool completely. Add ricotta chesse, egg and black pepper to taste and mix to combine. Spoon filling into pastry case, sprinkle with sesame seeds and bake at 180°C/350°F/Gas 4 for 25-30 minutes or until pastry is cooked and filling heated through.

Serves 4

Lentil and Spinach Quiche

Mixed Bean and Feta Salad

MIXED BEAN AND FETA SALAD

375 g/12 oz mixed dried beans of
choice, soaked overnight and drained
125 g/4 oz green beans, halved and
blanched
125 g/4 oz canned sweet corn kernels,
drained
2 carrots, cut into matchsticks
1 red onion, sliced
60 g/2 oz feta cheese, cubed

DRESSING
1/4 cup/60 mL/2 fl oz olive oil
2 tablespoons lemon juice or vinegar
1 teaspoon dried tarragon
freshly ground black pepper

1   Place dried beans in a saucepan,
cover with cold water and bring to the
boil. Boil for 10 minutes, then reduce
heat and simmer for 45 minutes or until
beans are tender. Drain and set aside.

2   Place mixed beans, green beans,
sweet corn, carrots, onion and feta
cheese in a salad bowl and toss to
combine.

3   To make dressing, place oil, lemon
juice or vinegar, tarragon and black
pepper to taste in a bowl and whisk to
combine. Spoon dressing over salad and
toss. Cover and refrigerate for 1 hour or
until ready to serve.

Serves 6

To blanch green beans,
drop into boiling water for
30-60 seconds, drain then
refresh under cold running
water. Allow this salad to
marinate for at least an
hour before serving to allow
flavours mellow.

33

Family Favourites

IRRESISTIBLE PIZZA

Oven temperature
200°C, 400°F, Gas 6

For a quick scone dough
pizza base: Rub 45 g/1¹/₂ oz
butter into 3 cups/375 g/
12 oz self-raising flour. Stir in
1 cup/250 mL/8 fl oz water
and ¹/₂ cup/125 mL/4 fl oz
milk and mix to make a soft
dough. Knead lightly and
press into rounds 5 mm/¹/₄ in
thick. Top and bake as
directed.

8 small pitta bread rounds
¹/₂ cup/125 mL/4 fl oz tomato paste
(pureé)
1 onion, thinly sliced
125 g/4 oz cabanossi sausage
(kabanos), sliced
60 g/2 oz sliced salami, chopped
6 button mushrooms, sliced
1 red or green pepper, seeded and
chopped
30 g/1 oz pitted black olives, sliced
2 tablespoons chopped fresh herbs of
your choice
250 g/8 oz grated mozzarella cheese

Place pitta bread rounds on baking
trays and spread with tomato paste
(pureé). Top each with equal quantities
of onion, cabanossi (kabanos), salami,
mushrooms, red or green pepper, olives,
herbs and mozzarella cheese. Bake for
10-15 minutes or until cheese melts
and bases are crisp.

Makes 8

FISH AND CRISPY CHIPS

1 kg/2 lb potatoes, peeled and cut
into chunky slices
vegetable oil for deep frying
6 firm white boneless fish fillets

BEER BATTER
1 cup/125 g/4 oz flour
1 cup/250 mL/8 fl oz beer
2 eggs, separated
1 tablespoon vegetable oil

When deep frying, use
enough oil to fill a large
saucepan to two-thirds full.
Cook small batches of food
at a time to avoid
dangerous spill-overs.
Double-cooking chips as
described in this recipe
ensures that they are crisp
and golden everytime.

1   To make batter, sift flour into a bowl
and make a well in the centre. Place
beer, egg yolks and oil in a separate
bowl and whisk to combine. Pour into
well in flour and mix to make a smooth
batter. Set aside to stand for 20 minutes.

2   Place potato slices in a bowl of cold
water and soak for 10 minutes. Drain
and pat dry on a teatowel or absorbent
kitchen paper. Heat oil in a large

saucepan until a cube of bread browns
in 50 seconds. Cook chips, in batches,
for 5 minutes or until soft but not
brown. Drain well on absorbent
kitchen paper and set aside until just
prior to serving.

3   Reheat oil as described above and
cook chips for 5 minutes or until
golden and crisp. Drain on absorbent
kitchen paper and keep warm in a low
oven while cooking the fish.

4   Place egg whites in a clean bowl and
beat until stiff peaks form. Fold egg
whites into batter. Reheat oil as
described above. Dip fish into batter,
draining off excess and cook 2 fillets for
4-5 minutes or until crisp and golden.
Drain on absorbent kitchen paper.
Serve immediately with chips.

Serves 6

FAMILY ROAST

1.5 kg/3 lb piece fresh silverside
1 tablespoon olive oil
freshly ground black pepper

ROAST VEGETABLES
6 large potatoes, halved
6 pieces pumpkin or 3 parsnips,
halved
6 onions, peeled
^{1}/$_4$ cup/60 mL/2 fl oz olive oil

MUSHROOM GRAVY
1 cup/250 mL/8 fl oz red wine or
beef stock
60 g/2 oz button mushrooms, sliced
^{1}/$_2$ teaspoon dried tarragon

1 Place beef on a wire rack set in a flameproof roasting dish or tin. Brush beef with 1 tablespoon oil and sprinkle with black pepper to taste. Bake for 1-1^1/$_4$ hours for medium rare or until cooked to your liking.

2 For vegetables, place potatoes, pumpkin or parsnips and onions in a large saucepan, cover with water and bring to the boil. Reduce heat and simmer for 3 minutes, then drain. Arrange vegetables in a baking dish and brush with ^{1}/$_4$ cup/60 mL/2 fl oz oil. Bake, turning once during cooking, for 45 minutes or until vegetables are tender and browned.

3 To make gravy, transfer roast to a serving platter, cover with foil and rest for 15 minutes. Stir wine or stock, mushrooms, tarragon and black pepper to taste into meat juices in roasting dish or tin and place over a medium heat. Bring to the boil, stirring to loosen sediment, then reduce heat and simmer until sauce reduces and thickens. Slice beef and serve with vegetables and gravy.

Serves 6-8

Oven temperature
180°C, 350°F, Gas 4

Yorkshire pudding and horseradish are traditional accompaniments to beef. To make Yorkshire pudding, sift ^{3}/$_4$ cup/90 g/3 oz flour and ^{1}/$_4$ teaspoon salt into a bowl, then whisk in ^{1}/$_2$ cup/ 125 mL/4 fl oz water and 2 eggs to make a smooth batter. Pour about ^{1}/$_2$ teaspoon of dripping or vegetable oil into six deep patty cake or muffin tins and heat at 220°C/ 425°F/Gas 7 for 3 minutes or until hot and sizzling. Divide batter between tins and bake for 15-20 minutes or until puffed and golden.

Plates Villeroy & Boch

TUNA AND VEGETABLE BAKE

Oven temperature
180°C, 350°F, Gas 4

125 g/4 oz small pasta shapes of your
choice, cooked and drained
440 g/14 oz canned tuna, drained
and flaked
500 g/1 lb mixed vegetables of
your choice, cooked
1 onion, thinly sliced

MUSTARD SAUCE
60 g/2 oz butter
2 tablespoons flour
2 cups/500 mL/16 fl oz milk
$^{1}/_{2}$ teaspoon dry mustard
freshly ground black pepper

CHEESY TOPPING
1 tomato, sliced
125 g/4 oz grated tasty cheese
(mature Cheddar)
$^{1}/_{4}$ cup/15 g/$^{1}/_{2}$ oz breadcrumbs,
made from stale bread

1   Layer pasta, tuna, vegetables and
onion in a greased large ovenproof dish
and set aside.

2   To make sauce, melt butter in a
saucepan over a medium heat, add
flour and cook, stirring, for 1 minute.
Remove pan from heat and gradually
blend in milk, mustard and black
pepper to taste. Return to heat and
cook, stirring constantly, for 5 minutes
or until sauce boils and thickens.
Simmer, stirring constantly, for
3 minutes. Pour sauce over tuna mixture.

3   For topping, arrange tomato slices
over sauce. Sprinkle with cheese
and breadcrumbs and bake for
30-35 minutes or until top is golden.

Serves 4

Any combination of diced,
cooked and well drained
fresh or frozen vegetables
may be used. Alternatively,
use 440 g/14 oz canned
mixed vegetables, drained.
Reconstituted full cream
powdered milk may be
used in place of fresh milk
in cooked sauces for extra
economy.

BEAN AND SAUSAGE COBBLER

Oven temperature
190°C, 375°F, Gas 5

1 tablespoon vegetable oil
1 onion, chopped
6 pork or beef sausages
440 g/14 oz canned tomatoes,
undrained and mashed
315 g/10 oz canned red kidney beans,
rinsed and drained
250 g/8 oz broccoli florets
1 green pepper, chopped
$^{1}/_{2}$ teaspoon chilli powder
freshly ground black pepper

CHEESY SCONE TOPPING
350 g/11 oz packet scone mix
125 g/4 oz grated tasty cheese
(mature Cheddar)

1   Heat oil in a frying pan over a
medium heat, add onion and cook,
stirring, for 5 minutes or until onion is
soft. Add sausages and cook, turning

several times for 10 minutes or until
sausages are almost cooked through and
brown on all sides. Slice sausages
lengthwise and place in a casserole
dish. Add onion.

2   Stir tomatoes, red kidney beans,
broccoli, green pepper, chilli powder
and black pepper to taste into sausage
mixture, cover and bake for 30 minutes.

3   To make topping, make up scone
mix according to packet directions.
Roll out dough to 1 cm/$^{1}/_{2}$ in thick
and using a 7.5 cm/3 in cutter, cut out
rounds. Place rounds on top of sausage
mixture, sprinkle with cheese and
bake for 30 minutes or until topping
is cooked and cheese melts.

Serves 4

Rather than using a packet
scone mix any basic scone
mixture could be used for
the topping in this recipe.
For a quick recipe see hint
on page 36.

APRICOT CHICKEN

Oven temperature
180°C, 350°F, Gas 4

Chicken can be one of the least expensive bases for a main course, especially if you purchase the more economical chicken pieces such as legs, wings or thigh fillets.

1.5 kg/ 3 lb chicken pieces
1 onion, sliced
45 g/1^1/$_2$ oz packet French onion or chicken noodle soup
2 teaspoons curry powder
440 g/14 oz canned apricot halves in natural juice
^{1}/$_4$ cup/60 mL/2 fl oz white wine or water

1 Arrange chicken pieces in a large ovenproof dish. Scatter with onion, then sprinkle with soup mix and curry powder.

2 Combine apricots with juice and wine or water, pour over chicken and mix to combine. Cover and bake for 1-1^1/$_4$ hours or until chicken is tender.

Serves 6

CHICKEN STROGANOFF

Chicken is a cheaper choice for protein and works just as well as red meat in classic dishes such as this. Serve with rice or pasta and a green salad. If you prefer a saucier mixture, add a little chicken stock or a 440 g/14 oz can of undrained mashed tomatoes at same time as the mushrooms.

2 tablespoons olive oil
1 onion, sliced
1 clove garlic, crushed
8 chicken thigh fillets or 4 boneless chicken breast fillets, sliced
125 g/4 oz button mushrooms, sliced
1^1/$_4$ cups/315 g/10 oz sour cream
^{1}/$_4$ cup/60 mL/2 fl oz tomato paste (pureé)
^{1}/$_2$ teaspoon paprika
freshly ground black pepper
2 spring onions, chopped or chopped fresh parsley

1 Heat oil in a frying pan over a medium heat, add onion and garlic and cook, stirring, for 4-5 minutes or until onion is tender. Add chicken and cook, stirring, for 3-4 minutes or until chicken is just cooked. Add mushrooms and cook, stirring, for 2 minutes longer.

2 Stir sour cream, tomato paste (pureé), paprika and black pepper to taste into pan, bring to simmering and simmer for 5 minutes or until sauce thickens. Sprinkle with spring onions or parsley and serve immediately.

Serves 6

Apricot Chicken, Chicken Stroganoff

CRUNCHY FAMILY MEATLOAF

Oven temperature
180°C, 350°F, Gas 4

For a delicious new meal from leftover meatloaf, top each slice of meatloaf with a slice of tomato and a little grated tasty cheese (mature Cheddar) and grill until cheese melts. Serve between slices of toasted bread or focaccia bread. Use this seasoned mince mixture to make perfect hamburgers – another family favourite! Shape into flat patties and fry in a little oil until cooked through and golden on both sides.

750 g/1^1/$_2$ lb beef mince
1 potato, grated
1 carrot, grated
1 onion, finely chopped
^{1}/$_2$ cup/30 g/1 oz breadcrumbs, made from stale bread
1 egg, beaten
2 tablespoons tomato sauce or fruit chutney
1 teaspoon dried mixed herbs
freshly ground black pepper

CRUNCHY TOPPING
^{1}/$_4$ cup/60 mL/2 fl oz tomato sauce mixed with 2 tablespoons Worcestershire sauce
^{1}/$_2$ cup/30 g/1 oz breadcrumbs, made from stale bread
60 g/2 oz butter, melted

1 Place beef, potato, carrot, onion, breadcrumbs, egg, tomato sauce or chutney, herbs and black pepper to taste in a bowl and mix well to combine.

2 Press mixture into a lightly greased 11 x 21 cm/4^1/$_2$ x 8^1/$_2$ in loaf tin and bake for 1 hour or until cooked.

3 Drain off excess juices and turn meatloaf onto a lightly greased baking tray. Brush with tomato sauce mixture. Combine breadcrumbs and butter, sprinkle over meatloaf and bake for 15-20 minutes longer or until topping is crisp and golden. Serve hot or cold.

Serves 6

Plate Villeroy & Boch

Left: Crunchy Family Meatloaf
Above: Salmon Patties

SALMON PATTIES

500 g/1 lb potatoes, chopped
220 g/7 oz canned pink salmon,
drained and flaked
1 onion, finely chopped
2 tablespoons chopped fresh parsley
1 egg, beaten
1 tablespoon lemon juice or vinegar
freshly ground black pepper
seasoned flour
vegetable oil for shallow-frying

1 Place potatoes in saucepan and cover with cold water. Bring to the boil, then reduce heat, cover and simmer for 10 minutes or until potatoes are tender. Drain potatoes, place in a bowl and mash.

2 Add salmon, onion, parsley, egg, lemon juice or vinegar and black pepper to taste and mix well to combine. Shape mixture into eight patties and roll in flour to coat. Shake off excess flour. Place patties on a plate lined with plastic food wrap and refrigerate for 15 minutes or until firm.

3 Heat oil in a frying pan over a medium heat add patties and cook for 2-3 minutes each side or until golden and heated through. Drain on absorbent kitchen paper.

Serves 4

Waste not want not – when shallow-frying, use only enough oil to cover the base of the frying pan. Vinegar can be used in place of lemon juice. A little grated lemon rind is also a tasty addition to the patty mixture. Canned pink salmon is the economical choice rather than red salmon for simple patties such as these.

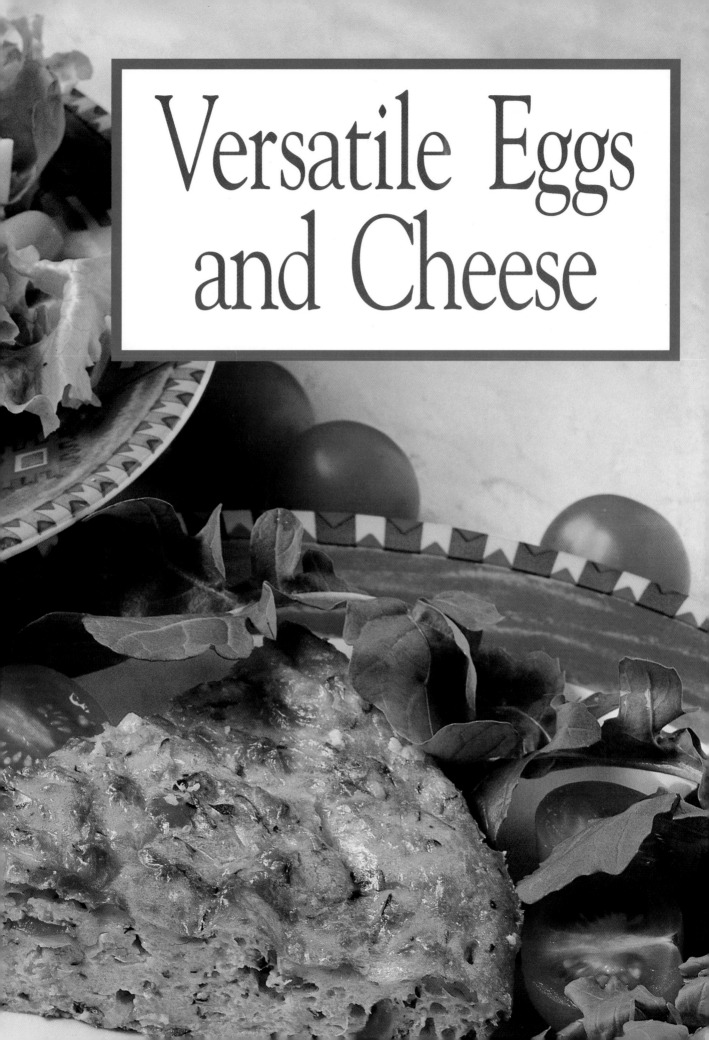

Versatile Eggs and Cheese

*Previous pages: Salad Niçoise,
Vegetable and Cheese Pie*

SALAD NIÇOISE

For a complete meal, serve with crusty fresh or toasted French bread.
A few anchovies and shavings of Parmesan cheese are delicious additions to this dish. Always buy the form of the product that best fits your menu. Less expensive shredded or flaked tuna is the perfect choice for a salad such as this – it's lower priced because of appearance, not quality. Feta cheese makes a delicious and more gourmet alternative to tasty cheese (mature Cheddar).

lettuce leaves of choice

TUNA SALAD
440 g/14 oz canned tuna, drained and flaked
125 g/4 oz canned artichoke hearts, drained and sliced (optional)
125 g/4 oz tasty cheese (mature Cheddar), cubed
4 hard-boiled eggs, sliced
2 potatoes, cooked and sliced
2 tomatoes, sliced
1 onion, sliced
250 g/8 oz green beans, cooked
45 g/1 1/2 oz stuffed olives, sliced

NIÇOISE DRESSING
1/4 cup/60 mL/2 fl oz olive oil
2 tablespoons vinegar
1 clove garlic, crushed
1/2 teaspoon Dijon mustard
freshly ground black pepper

1 To make salad, place tuna, artichokes, if using, cheese, eggs, potatoes, tomatoes, onion, beans and olives in a large bowl and toss to combine.

2 To make dressing, place oil, vinegar, garlic, mustard and black pepper to taste in a screwtop jar and shake well to combine. Spoon dressing over salad and toss lightly.

3 Line a large serving platter with lettuce leaves and top with salad.

Serves 6

VEGETABLE AND CHEESE PIE

Oven temperature
180°C, 350°F, Gas 4

For a complete meal serve wedges of this easy family-style pie with salad and crusty bread. It is also delicious cold so makes an excellent picnic dish or leftovers can be used for packed lunches.

3 zucchini (courgettes), grated
125 g/4 oz canned creamed sweet corn
1 stalk celery, chopped
1 onion, chopped
1/2 red or green pepper, chopped
60 g/2 oz grated tasty cheese (mature Cheddar)
1/2 cup/60 g/2 oz self-raising flour
4 eggs
2 tablespoons vegetable oil
1/2 teaspoon dried oregano
freshly ground black pepper

1 Place zucchini (courgettes), sweet corn, celery, onion, red or green pepper, cheese and flour in a large bowl and mix to combine.

2 Place eggs, oil, oregano and black pepper to taste into a separate bowl and whisk to combine. Stir egg mixture into vegetable mixture and spoon into a lightly greased 23 cm/9 in round ovenproof dish. Bake for 40-45 minutes or until pie is firm and top is golden.

Serves 6

Baked Ricotta with Vegetables

BAKED RICOTTA WITH VEGETABLES

1 kg/2 lb ricotta cheese, drained
2 tablespoons chopped fresh
mixed herbs
freshly ground black pepper
olive oil
2 tablespoons paprika
1.5 kg/3 lb assorted fresh vegetables,
sliced
focaccia bread or French bread stick,
sliced and toasted

1 Place ricotta cheese in a colander set over a bowl, cover with plastic food wrap and drain in the refrigerator for 2-3 hours or overnight.

2 Place ricotta cheese, herbs and black pepper to taste in a bowl and mix to combine. Press mixture into a greased 11 x 21 cm/4^1/$_2$ x 8^1/$_2$ in loaf tin and bake for 1 hour or until firm.

3 Turn loaf onto a lightly greased baking tray, brush lightly with oil, sprinkle with paprika and bake for 10 minutes or golden. Set aside to cool.

4 Brush vegetables lightly with oil and cook under a preheated hot grill or on a barbecue, turning several times, for 5-10 minutes or until vegetables are tender. To serve, cut ricotta loaf in slices and accompany with vegetables and toasted bread.

Serves 6

Oven temperature
180°C, 350°F, Gas 4

Try a combination of parsley, chives and basil for the herbs. For the vegetables, use eggplant (aubergines), carrots, tomatoes, green or red peppers, zucchini (courgettes), onions, sweet potato, leeks or any vegetables in plentiful supply and therefore reasonably priced.
The ricotta can be served hot, warm or cold.

SALMON ROULADE

Oven temperature
200°C, 400°F, Gas 6

Roulades are an economical and elegant dish for brunches and light luncheons. They can be made several hours ahead of time. Place on a serving dish or baking tray and cover with foil, then reheat, if desired, at 180°C/350°F/ Gas 4 for 10-15 minutes. Serve as a first course or as a main meal with salad and crusty bread.

60 g/2 oz butter
$^{1}/_{3}$ cup/45 g/1$^{1}/_{2}$ oz flour
1 cup/250 mL/8 fl oz milk
4 eggs, separated
100 g/3$^{1}/_{2}$ oz grated tasty cheese (mature Cheddar)
freshly ground black pepper

SALMON FILLING
220 g/7 oz canned pink salmon, drained and flaked
$^{1}/_{2}$ cup/125 g/4 oz sour cream
4 spring onions, chopped
2 teaspoons finely grated lemon rind
2 tablespoons lemon juice

CUCUMBER YOGURT SAUCE
1 cup/200 g/6$^{1}/_{2}$ oz natural yogurt
1 cucumber, peeled, seeded and chopped
1 clove garlic, crushed
1 tablespoon lemon juice
freshly ground black pepper

1 Melt butter in a saucepan over a medium heat, stir in flour and cook for 1 minute. Remove pan from heat and gradually stir in milk. Return pan to heat and cook, stirring, for 4-5 minutes or until sauce boils and thickens. Remove from heat and beat in egg yolks, one at a time. Add cheese and black pepper to taste and stir until cheese melts and mixture is smooth. Transfer sauce to a bowl.

2 Place egg whites in a clean bowl and beat until stiff peaks form. Fold egg whites into sauce. Spoon roulade mixture into a greased and lined 26 x 32 cm/10$^{1}/_{2}$ x 12$^{3}/_{4}$ in Swiss roll tin and bake for 10-12 minutes or until puffed and golden.

3 To make filling, place salmon, sour cream, spring onions, lemon rind and lemon juice in a bowl and mix to combine. Set aside.

4 Turn roulade onto a wire rack covered with a clean teatowel and roll up from short end. Hold for 30 seconds, then unroll and carefully remove paper. Spread filling evenly over roulade and roll up again.

5 To make sauce, place yogurt, cucumber, garlic, lemon juice and black pepper to taste in a bowl and mix to combine. Serve roulade warm or at room temperature accompanied by sauce.

Serves 6

Plate Waterford Wedgwood

Left: Samon Roulade
Right: Spicy Cheese Soufflé

Spicy Cheese Souffle

90 g/3 oz butter
$^{1}/_{3}$ cup/45 g/1$^{1}/_{2}$ oz flour
1$^{1}/_{2}$ cups/375 mL/12 fl oz milk
pinch cayenne pepper
$^{1}/_{4}$ teaspoon dry mustard
freshly ground black pepper
6 eggs, separated
185 g/6 oz grated tasty cheese
(mature Cheddar)
2 tablespoons chopped mixed
fresh herbs or 2 teaspoons dried
mixed herbs

Serves 4

1 Melt butter in a saucepan over a medium heat, stir in flour and cook for 1 minute. Remove pan from heat and gradually blend in milk, cayenne pepper, mustard and black pepper to taste. Return pan to heat and cook, stirring constantly, for 5-6 minutes or until mixture boils and thickens. Simmer for 3 minutes.

2 Remove pan from heat and beat in egg yolks, one at a time. Add cheese and herbs and stir until cheese is melts and mixture is smooth. Set aside to cool slightly.

3 Place egg whites in a clean bowl and beat until stiff peaks form. Fold egg whites into cheese mixture. Spoon soufflé mixture into a greased 8 cup/2 litre/3$^{1}/_{2}$ pt ovenproof dish and bake for 35-40 minutes or until soufflé is puffed and golden. Serve immediately.

Oven temperature
180°C, 350°F, Gas 4

Any 8 cup/2 litre/3$^{1}/_{2}$ pt oven-to-table dish is suitable for a making a family soufflé, but if the classic high-top look is preferred, use a 6 cup/1.5 litre/2$^{1}/_{2}$ pt straight-sided dish and extend its capacity by tying a double layer of greased, baking paper around its rim with string to make a collar. Save a slumped soufflé by turning it out of the dish into a heatproof bowl. Drizzle the top with a little cream, sprinkle with extra cheese and bake for 10 minutes or until cheese melts.

EGGS FLORENTINE

90 g/3 oz butter
1/3 cup/45 g/11/2 oz flour
2 cups/500 mL/16 fl oz milk
125 g/4 oz grated tasty cheese
(mature Cheddar)
freshly ground black pepper
250 g/8 oz frozen chopped spinach,
thawed
6 eggs
30 g/1 oz grated Parmesan cheese

The ingredients for this dish are almost always on hand, making it ideal for unexpected guests. Fresh spinach can be used in place of the frozen if you wish, if using fresh spinach, roughly chop 1 bunch/ 500 g/1 lb English spinach and cook in a little butter in a frying pan over a medium heat until wilted. Drain and use as directed.

1 Melt 60 g/2 oz butter in a saucepan over a medium heat, stir in flour and cook for 1 minute. Remove pan from heat and gradually blend in milk. Return pan to heat and cook, stirring, for 5-6 minutes or until sauce boils and thickens. Simmer for 3 minutes.

2 Remove pan from heat, add tasty cheese (mature Cheddar) and black pepper to taste and stir until cheese melts and sauce is smooth. Cover surface of sauce with plastic food wrap and set aside to cool.

3 Squeeze excess liquid from spinach by pressing between two plates. Divide spinach between six 1 cup/250 mL/ 8 fl oz capacity ovenproof ramekins. Using the back of a tablespoon, make a depression in spinach.

4 Break an egg into each depression, then spoon sauce over eggs, sprinkle with Parmesan cheese and dot with remaining butter. Bake for 15-20 minutes or until golden. Serve immediately.

Serves 6

Plate Villeroy & Boch

APPLE AND ONION TART

Left: Eggs Florentine
Above: Apple and Onion Tart

155 g/5 oz prepared puff pastry
30 g/1 oz butter
3 large onions, sliced
2 green eating apples, cored, peeled
and sliced
185 g/6 oz blue cheese, crumbled

1   Roll out pastry to form a rectangle
20 x 30 cm/8 x 12 in and place on a
lightly greased baking tray. Set aside.

2   Melt butter in a frying pan over a
medium heat, add onions and cook,
stirring for 10 minutes or until onions
are golden and caramelised. Remove
onions from pan and set aside to cool.

3   Add apples to same pan and cook,
turning several times, for 3 minutes or
until lightly browned. Remove apples
from pan and set aside to cool.

4   Arrange apples over pastry leaving a
2 cm/^{3}/4 in border, then scatter with
onions and blue cheese. Bake for
15-20 minutes or until pastry is puffed
and golden.

Serves 4

Oven temperature
200°C, 400°F, Gas 6

For a complete meal, serve
with a tossed green salad
and crusty bread.

SAVOURY QUICHE

Oven temperature
200°C, 400°F, Gas 6

2 cups/250 g/8 oz flour
90 g/3 oz butter, chopped
2-3 tablespoons iced water

HAM AND PEPPER FILLING
30 g/1 oz butter
90 g/3 oz ham or bacon, sliced
3 spring onions, chopped
1 leek, sliced
$^1/_2$ red or green pepper, chopped
2 eggs
$^1/_2$ cup/125 mL/4 fl oz milk
1 tablespoon snipped fresh chives
freshly ground black pepper
60 g/2 oz grated tasty cheese
(mature Cheddar)

Served hot or cold with salad and crusty bread, a quiche is an ecomomical main course for a light luncheon or casual dinner. If the budget allows, use 250 g/8 oz commercially prepared frozen shortcrust pastry and omit step 1.

1 Place flour in a bowl and rub in butter with fingertips until the mixture resembles coarse breadcrumbs. Mix in enough water to form a soft dough. Knead dough gently until smooth, wrap in plastic food wrap and refrigerate for 30 minutes.

2 Roll out pastry to 5 mm/$^1/_4$ in thick and use to line the base and sides of a lightly greased 20 cm/8 in flan tin. Line pastry case with nonstick baking paper, fill with uncooked rice and bake for 15 minutes. Remove paper and rice and bake for 10 minutes longer or until pastry is golden. Set aside to cool.

3 To make filling, melt butter in a frying pan over a medium heat, add ham or bacon, spring onions, leek and red or green pepper and cook, stirring, for 5 minutes or until leek is tender. Spoon mixture into pastry case.

4 Place eggs, milk, chives and black pepper to taste in a bowl and whisk to combine. Pour egg mixture evenly over vegetable mixture and sprinkle with cheese. Reduce oven temperature to 180°C/350°F/Gas 4 and bake for 25-30 minutes or until filling is set. Stand for 10 minutes before serving.

Serves 6

POTATO AND VEGETABLE BAKE

Oven temperature
180°C, 350°F, Gas 4

4 potatoes, thinly sliced
500 g/1 lb sweet potato, thinly sliced
3 parsnips, thinly sliced
1 onion, thinly sliced
$^1/_2$ teaspoon ground nutmeg
freshly ground black pepper
1 cup/250 mL/8 fl oz cream (double)
125 g/4 oz grated tasty cheese
(mature Cheddar)

Pumpkin or carrot may be used in place of the sweet potato in this simple side dish for meats, chicken or fish.

1 Arrange potatoes, sweet potato, parsnips and onion in alternate layers in a greased, shallow ovenproof dish. Sprinkle each layer with a little nutmeg and black pepper to taste.

2 Pour cream evenly over vegetables and bake for 30 minutes. Sprinkle with cheese and bake for 20-25 minutes longer or until vegetables are tender.

Serves 6

Savoury Quiche, Potato and Vegetable Bake

Above: Fluffy Omelette
Right: Potato and Leek Frittata

FLUFFY OMELETTE

2 eggs, separated
1 teaspoon snipped fresh chives
freshly ground black pepper
30 g/1 oz grated cheese of your choice
15 g/¹/₂ oz butter

BACON AND MUSHROOM
FILLING
15 g/¹/₂ oz butter
1 rasher bacon, chopped
6 button mushrooms, chopped
¹/₄ red pepper, chopped
1 teaspoon chopped fresh dill

Yesterday's leftovers can be today's main course when used as fillings for this simple omelette mixture. Serve omelette with a tossed green salad or steamed vegetables.

1 To make filling, melt butter in a frying pan over a medium heat, add bacon and mushrooms and cook, stirring, for 5 minutes or until bacon and mushrooms are cooked. Add red pepper and cook for 2-3 minutes longer. Stir in dill, remove filling from pan and set aside.

2 Place egg yolks, chives and black pepper to taste in a bowl and whisk to combine. Stir in cheese.

3 Place egg whites in a clean bowl and beat until stiff peaks form. Fold egg whites into egg yolk mixture.

4 Melt butter in an omelette pan over a medium heat. Add egg mixture to pan and cook, without stirring for 2-3 minutes or until edges of mixture just begin to set. Place pan under a preheated medium grill and cook for 1-2 minutes or until top is golden. Top with filling, fold in half and serve immediately.

Serves 1

POTATO AND LEEK FRITTATA

2 tablespoons olive oil
1 large potato, thinly sliced
2 leeks, thinly sliced
2 rashers bacon, chopped
6 eggs
1/2 cup/125 mL/4 fl oz milk
3 tablespoons grated Parmesan cheese
freshly ground black pepper

1   Heat oil in a large frying pan over a low heat, add potato, leeks and bacon and cook, stirring, for 8-10 minutes or until potato is tender.

2   Place eggs, milk, Parmesan cheese and black pepper to taste in a bowl and whisk to combine. Pour egg mixture over potato mixture and cook over a low heat for 6 minutes or until egg mixture is just set.

3   Place pan under a preheated hot grill and cook until top of frittata is golden. Serve hot, warm or cold cut into wedges.

Serves 4

Herbs of your choice and other ingredients such as sliced spicy sausage, mushrooms, tomatoes or olives can be added to the potato mixture for a delicious light meal. Serve with crusty bread and salad.

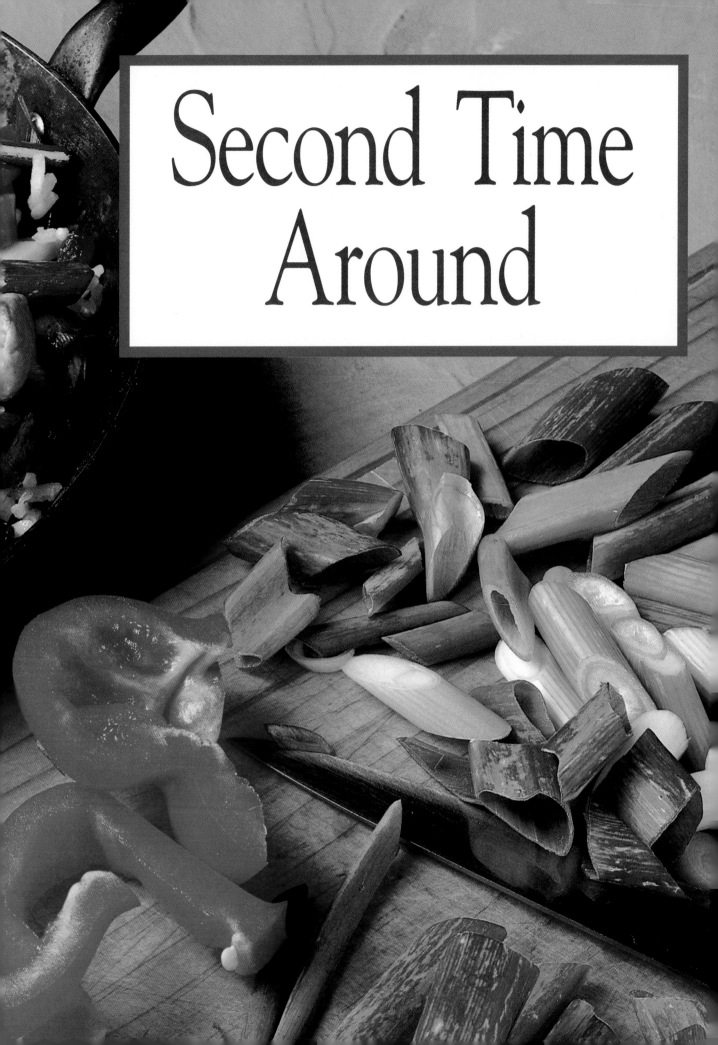

Second Time Around

NASI GORENG

^{1}/4 cup/60 mL/2 fl oz vegetable oil
1 onion, sliced
3 spring onions, chopped
250 g/8 oz diced pork
125 g/4 oz shelled uncooked prawns
(optional)
4 cups/750 g/1^1/2 lb cooked rice or
2 cups/440 g/14 oz raw rice, cooked
1 red pepper, chopped
45 g/1^1/2 oz sultanas or raisins
45 g/1^1/2 oz cashews or peanuts
(optional)
1 teaspoon chopped fresh red chilli
2 tablespoons soy sauce

CHINESE OMELETTE
2 eggs
2 teaspoons water
freshly ground black pepper

Chilli sauce can be used in place of the chopped fresh chilli if you wish. For something different garnish with sliced tomato, shredded lettuce or fried onion rings instead of omelette strips.

1 To make omelette, place eggs, water and black pepper to taste in a bowl and whisk to combine. Heat a lightly greased wok or frying pan over a medium heat, add half the egg mixture and tilt pan to thinly coat base. Cook for 1-2 minutes or until underside of omelette is set, flip omelette and cook for 10 seconds. Remove and set aside to cool. Use remaining egg mixture to make a second omelette. Stack omelettes, roll up and cut into fine shreds. Set aside.

2 Heat half the oil in a wok or large frying pan over a medium heat, add onion and spring onions and stir-fry for 3-4 minutes or until onion is tender. Add pork and stir-fry for 2-3 minutes. Add prawns, if using, and stir-fry for 1-2 minutes longer or until prawns change colour. Remove mixture from pan and set aside.

3 Heat remaining oil in same pan, add rice, red pepper, sultanas or raisins, cashews or peanuts, if using, chilli and soy sauce and stir-fry for 2 minutes. Return pork mixture to pan and stir-fry for 1 minute or until heated through. Top with omelette strips and serve immediately.

Serves 4

CRISPY PASTA

60 g/2 oz butter
500 g/1 lb cooked pasta of
your choice
125 g/4 oz grated tasty cheese
(mature Cheddar)
2 tablespoons grated Parmesan cheese
1 teaspoon dried mixed herbs

If using leftover cooked spaghetti, tagliatelle or fettuccine in this dish, chop it into bite-sized pieces. Sliced cold cooked sausage may also be tossed through the pasta.

Melt butter in a frying pan over a medium heat, add pasta, tasty cheese (mature Cheddar), Parmesan cheese and herbs and cook, stirring constantly, for 5 minutes or until hot and crispy. Serve immediately.

Serves 4

Sweet Meat Curry

SWEET MEAT CURRY

2 tablespoons olive oil
1 onion, chopped
1 clove garlic, crushed
1 tablespoon curry powder
1 teaspoon ground ginger
1 teaspoon chopped fresh red chilli
(optional)
2 carrots, chopped
2 stalks celery, chopped
1 apple, chopped
1 banana, sliced
2 tablespoons sultanas
2 tablespoons malt vinegar
1 tablespoon fruit chutney
2 teaspoons brown sugar
$2^1/2$ cups/600 mL/1 pt water
freshly ground black pepper
$^1/4$ cup/30 g/1 oz flour blended with
$^1/3$ cup/90 mL/3 fl oz water
500 g/1 lb chopped cooked beef, lamb,
pork or chicken

1   Heat oil in a large saucepan over a medium heat, add onion and garlic and cook, stirring, for 3-4 minutes or until onion is tender. Add curry powder, ginger and chilli, if using, and cook, for 1 minute or until fragrant.

2   Add carrots, celery, apple, banana, sultanas, vinegar, chutney and sugar and cook for 2-3 minutes. Stir in water and black pepper to taste and bring to the boil. Reduce heat, cover and simmer for 15-20 minutes or until vegetables are tender.

3   Stir flour mixture into curry and cook, stirring constantly, for 5 minutes or until mixture boils and thickens. Stir in meat and simmer for 5-10 minutes or until heated through.

Serves 6

Serve curry with rice and traditional Indian accompaniments such as pappadums, chutney and sambals, or boiled potatoes and steamed vegetables

SHEPHERD'S PIE

Oven temperature
180°C, 350°F, Gas 4

If cooked meat is unavailable, cook 500 g/1 lb beef mince with the onion in step 1 until browned. To expand the recipe further carrots, celery, mushrooms, green beans or cooked red kidney beans may be added to the meat mixture.

1 tablespoon olive oil
1 onion, chopped
500 g/1 lb chopped cooked beef, lamb, pork or chicken
1 tablespoon flour
$^{1}/_{2}$ cup/125 mL/4 fl oz beef stock or water
440 g/14 oz canned tomatoes, undrained and mashed
60 g/2 oz frozen peas
2 tablespoons tomato paste (purée)
1 tablespoon Worcestershire sauce

CHEESY POTATO TOPPING
3 potatoes, chopped
$^{1}/_{4}$ cup/60 mL/2 fl oz milk or cream (double)
freshly ground black pepper
60 g/2 oz grated tasty cheese (mature Cheddar)
$^{1}/_{4}$ cup/30 g/1 oz dried breadcrumbs

1 Heat oil in a frying pan over a medium heat, add onion and cook, stirring, for 2-3 minutes or until onion is tender. Stir in meat. Blend flour with a little of the stock or water to form a smooth paste. Stir flour mixture, remaining stock or water and tomatoes into pan and, stirring constantly, bring to the boil. Add peas, tomato paste (purée) and Worcestershire sauce and simmer, stirring frequently, for 5 minutes or until mixture thickens. Spoon mixture into a deep ovenproof dish or individual ramekins.

2 To make topping, place potatoes in saucepan, cover with cold water and bring to the boil. Reduce heat, cover and simmer for 15-20 minutes or until potatoes are tender. Drain well, add milk or cream and black pepper to taste and mash. Top meat mixture with potatoes, sprinkle with cheese and breadcrumbs and bake for 15-20 minutes or until top is golden.

Serves 4

Left: Shepherd's Pie
Right: Easy Stuffing for Vegetables

Plate Royal Worcester

EASY STUFFING FOR VEGETABLES

vegetables of your choice such as red or green peppers, eggplant (aubergines), tomatoes or zucchini (courgettes), prepared for stuffing

RICE STUFFING
2 tablespoons olive oil
1 onion, chopped
1 clove garlic, crushed
30 g/1 oz almonds, chopped
2 cups/375 g/12 oz cooked rice or
1 cup/220 g/7 oz raw rice, cooked
1 tomato, chopped
2 canned tomatoes, drained, seeded and pureéd
2 tablespoons currants, sultanas or chopped raisins
1 teaspoon finely grated lemon rind
1 tablespoon lemon juice
1 teaspoon dried basil
$^1/_2$ teaspoon dried dill
$^1/_4$ teaspoon ground allspice
freshly ground black pepper

1   To make stuffing, heat oil in a frying pan over a medium heat, add onion and garlic and cook, stirring, for 3-4 minutes or until onion is tender. Add almonds and cook for 1 minute longer.

2   Stir rice, tomato, puréed tomatoes, currants, sultanas or raisins, lemon rind, lemon juice, basil, dill, allspice and black pepper to taste in pan and bring to the boil. Reduce heat and simmer for 10 minutes or until mixture thickens.

3   Spoon stuffing into prepared vegetables and bake for 15-30 minutes or until vegetables are tender. Cooking time will depend on the vegetables used.

Makes enough stuffing for 4 servings

Oven temperature
180°C, 350°F, Gas 4

For a more substantial stuffing, add 250 g/8 oz chopped cooked meat or chicken to the mixture with the rice in step 2. The stuffing also makes a good filling for cabbage rolls. Blanch cabbage leaves until soft. Divide stuffing between leaves, wrap up and place in a shallow ovenproof dish. Purée 440 g/14 oz canned tomatoes with $^1/_2$ cup/ 125 mL/4 fl oz white wine, pour over cabbage rolls and bake for 25-30 minutes.

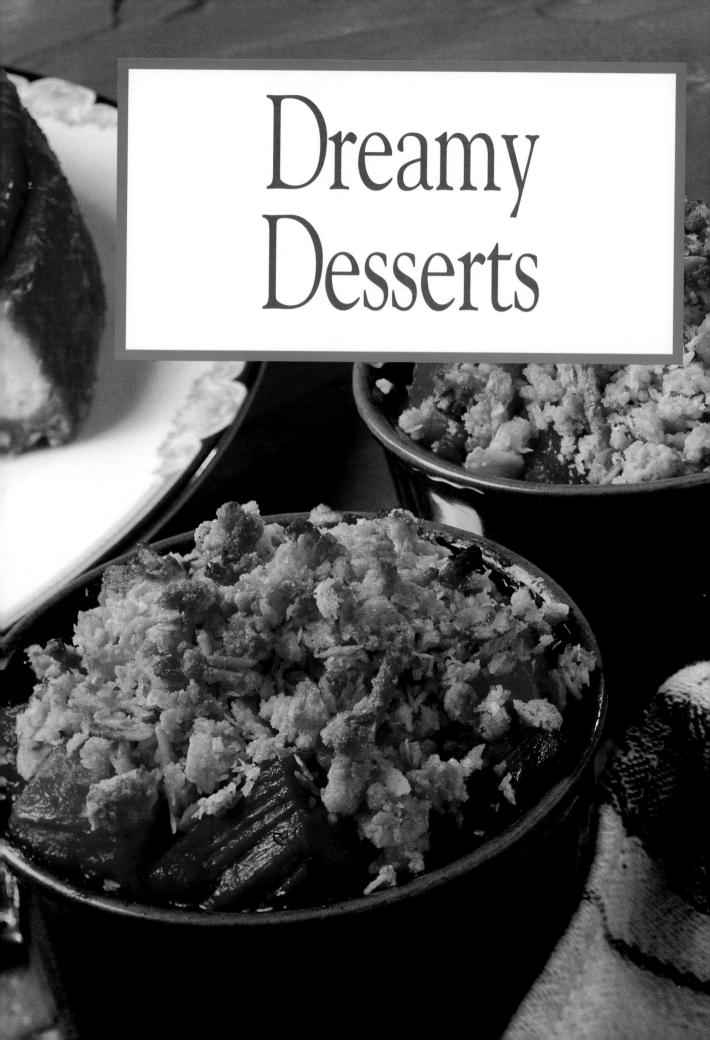

Dreamy
Desserts

Previous pages: Baked Yogurt Cheesecake, Rhubarb Crumble
Plate Waterford Wedgwood

BAKED YOGURT CHEESECAKE

Oven temperature
150°C, 300°F, Gas 2

For a special occasion decorate a cheesecake with whipped cream and fruit just prior to serving. Use this as a basic recipe to make other flavoured cheesecakes, you might like to add 440 g/14 oz drained canned fruit or blend 60 g/2 oz melted and cooled dark chocolate into the filling.

125 g/4 oz plain sweet biscuits, crushed
60 g/2 oz butter, melted
$1/2$ teaspoon ground cinnamon

YOGURT CHEESE FILLING
500 g/1 lb cream cheese, softened
1 cup/200 g/$6^1/2$ oz natural or fruit-flavoured yogurt of your choice
3 eggs
$1/2$ cup/125 mL/4 fl oz cream (double)
$1/2$ cup/100 g/$3^1/2$ oz caster sugar
3 teaspoons finely grated lemon rind

1 Place crushed biscuits, butter and cinnamon in a bowl and mix to combine. Press biscuit mixture over base of a well greased 23 cm/9 in springform tin and refrigerate until required.

2 To make filling, place cream cheese in a bowl and beat until smooth. Add yogurt, eggs, cream, sugar and lemon rind and beat to combine.

3 Pour filling into prepared tin and bake for 1 hour or until filling is firm. Cool cheesecake in tin to room temperature, then chill until ready to serve.

Serves 8

RHUBARB CRUMBLE

Oven temperature
180°C, 350°F, Gas 4

Other fruit such pears, fresh berries and canned fruit may be used to make a crumble. It is delicious served hot or cold with custard, cream or ice cream.

3 stalks rhubarb, trimmed and chopped
2 green cooking apples, peeled, cored and chopped
90 g/3 oz sultanas
60 g/2 oz slivered almonds
2 teaspoons finely grated lemon rind
2 tablespoons lemon juice
60 g/2 oz butter
$1/2$ cup/90 g/3 oz brown sugar
$1/4$ teaspoon ground cinnamon
$1/4$ teaspoon ground nutmeg

OATY COCONUT TOPPING
$1/2$ cup/60 g/2 oz flour, sifted
$1/2$ cup/45 g/$1^1/2$ oz rolled oats
$1/4$ cup/45 g/$1^1/2$ oz brown sugar
30 g/1 oz desiccated coconut
90 g/3 oz butter, softened and chopped

1 Place rhubarb, apples, sultanas, almonds, lemon rind and lemon juice in an ovenproof dish and mix to combine. Melt butter in a saucepan over a low heat, remove pan from heat and stir in sugar, cinnamon and nutmeg. Drizzle butter mixture over fruit in dish.

2 To make topping, place flour, rolled oats, sugar and coconut in a bowl and mix to combine. Rub in butter with fingertips until mixture resembles coarse breadcrumbs. Sprinkle topping over fruit and bake for 25-30 minutes or until fruit is tender and topping is golden.

Serves 4

Chocolate Pudding

CHOCOLATE PUDDING

1 cup/125 g/4 oz self-raising flour
$^{1}/_{4}$ cup/30 g/1 oz cocoa powder
$^{3}/_{4}$ cup/170 g/5$^{1}/_{2}$ oz caster sugar
$^{1}/_{2}$ cup/125 mL/4 fl oz milk
45 g/1$^{1}/_{2}$ oz butter, melted

CHOCOLATE SAUCE
$^{3}/_{4}$ cup/125 g/4 oz brown sugar
$^{1}/_{4}$ cup/30 g/1 oz cocoa powder, sifted
1$^{1}/_{4}$ cups/315 mL/10 fl oz hot water

1   Sift together flour and cocoa powder into a bowl. Add caster sugar and mix to combine. Make a well in the centre of the dry ingredients, add milk and butter and mix well to combine. Pour mixture into a greased 4 cup/1 litre/ 1$^{3}/_{4}$ pt capacity ovenproof dish.

2   To make sauce, place brown sugar and cocoa powder in a bowl. Gradually add water and mix until smooth. Carefully pour sauce over mixture in dish and bake for 40 minutes or until cake is cooked when tested with a skewer.

Serves 6

Oven temperature
180°C, 350°F, Gas 4

Serve scoops of pudding with some sauce from base of dish and accompany with a scoop of vanilla or chocolate ice cream.

Plate Villeroy & Boch

CHOCOLATE BROWNIE

Oven temperature
180°C, 350°F, Gas 4

185 g/6 oz dark chocolate, roughly
chopped
45 g/1^1/$_2$ oz butter, chopped
1 egg
^{1}/$_4$ cup/60 g/2 oz caster sugar
^{1}/$_2$ teaspoon vanilla essence
1 cup/125 g/4 oz self-raising flour,
sifted
1 cup/125 g/4 oz flour, sifted

CHOCOLATE COFFEE SAUCE
125 g/4 oz dark chocolate, roughly
chopped
60 g/2 oz butter
^{1}/$_4$ cup/60 mL/2 fl oz cream (double)
2 tablespoons brown sugar
1 teaspoon instant coffee powder

1   Place chocolate and butter in heatproof bowl over a suacepan of simmering water and heat, stirring, for 5 minutes or until chocolate melts and mixture is smooth.

2   Place egg, caster sugar and vanilla essence in a bowl and beat until mixture is thick and creamy. Beat in chocolate mixture, then fold in self-raising flour and flour. Spoon mixture into a lightly greased and lined 20 cm/ 8 in round cake tin and bake for 15-20 minutes or until cooked when tested with a skewer. Stand brownie in tin for 5 minutes before turning onto a wire to cool for 5-10 minutes.

3   To make sauce, place chocolate, butter, cream, brown sugar and coffee powder in a small saucepan and mix to combine. Heat over a medium heat, stirring constantly, for 4-5 minutes or until chocolate and butter melt and sauce is smooth. Serve brownie warm with sauce.

Serves 6

Caramelised Fruit with Almonds

Chocolate Brownie

CARAMELISED FRUIT WITH ALMONDS

440 g/14 oz canned peach halves,
drained
440 g/14 oz canned apricot halves,
drained
$^1/4$ cup/60 mL/2 fl oz brandy, rum or
fruit juice
$1^1/4$ cups/315 g/10 oz sour cream
$^1/2$ cup/90 g/3 oz brown sugar
3 tablespoons flaked almonds

1 Place peaches and apricots, cut side
up, in a shallow ovenproof dish. Pour
brandy, rum or fruit juice over fruit and
set aside to macerate for at least 30
minutes.

2 Fill fruit with sour cream, then
sprinkle with sugar and almonds. Place
under a preheated hot grill and cook
until sugar caramelises and almonds
brown. Serve immediately.

Serves 6

Any combination of fresh
chopped fruit and berries
may be used instead of the
canned fruit. Pick the
cheapest buy from the
fresh or canned varieties
available for this easy
family-style dessert.

The Thrifty Entertainer

GRILLED VEGETABLE SALAD

Previous pages: Grilled Vegetable Salad, Daube of Beef

4 slices bread, crusts removed, cubed
2 rashers bacon
3 baby eggplant (aubergines), sliced
1 red or green pepper, cut into thick
slices
2 tablespoons olive oil
lettuce leaves of your choice
1 onion, thinly sliced
60 g/2 oz grated Parmesan cheese

ZESTY DRESSING
$^1/_3$ cup/90 mL/3 fl oz olive oil
1 tablespoon cider vinegar
1 clove garlic, crushed
2 tablespoons lemon juice
2 teaspoons Worcestershire sauce
Tabasco sauce
freshly ground black pepper

For a vegetarian version of this recipe simply omit the bacon.

1 Place bread on a baking tray and bake for 10 minutes or until golden and crisp. Set aside to cool.

2 Cook bacon under a preheated hot grill for 3-4 minutes or until crisp. Drain on absorbent kitchen paper and chop. Set aside.

3 Brush eggplant (aubergines) and pepper with oil and cook under a preheated medium grill, brushing occasionally with oil, for 5 minutes each side or until golden and tender. Set aside to cool.

4 Arrange lettuce leaves on serving plates. Top with equal amounts of vegetables, onion and bacon.

5 To make dressing, place oil, vinegar, garlic, lemon juice, Worcestershire sauce, a dash of Tabasco sauce and black pepper to taste in a screwtop jar and shake well to combine. Just prior to serving, drizzle dressing over salad and sprinkle with croûtons and Parmesan cheese.

Serves 6

TOMATO AND BASIL BRUSCHETTA

Oven temperature
200°C, 400°F, Gas 6

$^1/_2$ cup/125 mL/4 fl oz olive oil
2 cloves garlic, crushed
1 French bread stick, sliced diagonally
3 tomatoes, finely chopped
3 tablespoons chopped fresh basil or
parsley
freshly ground black pepper

For a light meal, top bruschetta with a little grated Parmesan or mozzarella cheese and grill until cheese melts. Serve with a salad.

1 Combine oil and garlic. Brush bread slices liberally with oil mixture and place on an oiled baking tray. Bake for 10 minutes or until bread is golden. Set aside to cool.

2 Place tomatoes, basil or parsley and black pepper to taste in a bowl and mix to combine. Just prior to serving, top toasted bread slices with tomato mixture.

Serves 6

Tomato and Basil Bruschetta

DAUBE OF BEEF

1 kg/2 lb chuck or blade steak,
trimmed of all visible fat and cubed
$^1/_2$ cup/60 g/2 oz seasoned flour
$^1/_4$ cup/60 mL/2 fl oz olive oil
1 onion, chopped
1 clove garlic, crushed
1 leek, sliced
2 cups/500 mL/16 fl oz beef stock
1 cup/250 mL/8 fl oz red wine
1 teaspoon dried mixed herbs
freshly ground black pepper
1 bay leaf
few thin strips orange rind (optional)
2 zucchini (courgettes), sliced
1 large sweet potato, chopped
1 parsnip, sliced

1 Toss beef in flour. Shake off excess and set aside. Heat half the oil in a large frying pan over a medium heat and cook beef in batches for 3-4 minutes or until brown. Place in a casserole dish.

2 Heat remaining oil in same pan, add onion and garlic and cook over a medium heat, stirring, for 4-5 minutes. Add leek and cook for 2-3 minutes longer. Add vegetables to casserole dish.

3 Add stock, wine, herbs and black pepper to taste to pan and stirring, bring to the boil. Reduce heat and simmer until liquid reduces by half. Add stock mixture, bay leaf and orange rind, if using, to casserole dish and bake for 1$^1/_2$-2 hours or until beef is tender.

4 Add zucchini (courgettes), sweet potato and parsnip and cook for 30 minutes or until vegetables are tender.

Serves 4

Oven temperature
150°C, 300°F, Gas 2

To clean dirty leeks, slice off hard outer green leaves and cut in half lengthwise. Wash under cold running water to remove any grit that is caught between the layers. Drain well and use as required. When leeks are expensive, omit them and use an extra onion instead.

Plate Villeroy & Boch

HONEYED SQUID SALAD

6 small squid (calamari), cleaned and
sliced into rings
$1/4$ cup/30 g/1 oz flour
olive oil for shallow-frying
lettuce leaves of your choice
250 g/8 oz cherry tomatoes, halved
1 onion, thinly sliced

HONEY ORANGE DRESSING
$1/4$ cup/60 mL/2 fl oz olive oil
1 tablespoon orange juice
1 tablespoon vinegar
1 teaspoon honey
1 clove garlic, crushed
$1/4$ teaspoon mild mustard
freshly ground black pepper

To clean fresh squid (calamari), pull off tentacles, carefully taking with them the head, stomach and ink bag. Rub off the skin under cold running water. Slice tube (body) crosswise into rings. If fresh squid (calamari) is unavailable, use 375 g/ 12 oz frozen squid (calamari) rings instead.

1   To make dressing, place oil, orange juice, vinegar, honey, garlic, mustard and black pepper to taste in a screwtop jar and shake well to combine.

2   Dry squid (calamari) rings on absorbent kitchen paper. Toss in flour and shake off excess. Heat oil in a frying pan over a medium heat, add squid (calamari) and stir-fry for 1-2 minutes or until golden. Drain on absorbent kitchen paper.

3   Place lettuce leaves, tomatoes and onion in a bowl and toss. Divide lettuce mixture between serving plates, top with hot squid (calamari) and drizzle with dressing. Serve immediately.

Serves 4

MUSSELS IN CHILLI CREAM SAUCE

1 tablespoon olive oil
2 onions, sliced
2 cloves garlic, crushed
$1^1/4$ cups/315 mL/10 fl oz cream
(double)
440 g/14 oz canned tomatoes,
undrained and mashed
1 tablespoon chopped fresh basil or
1 teaspoon dried basil leaves
1 teaspoon chopped fresh red chilli
freshly ground black pepper
1.5 kg/3 lb mussels, scrubbed and
beards removed

Delicious served with crusty bread. Remove mussel beards by grasping the fuzzy fibres protruding from the shells and pulling. Scrub shells with a stiff brush under cold running water to remove all grit.

1   Heat oil in a saucepan over a medium heat, add onions and garlic and cook, stirring, for 5 minutes or until onions are tender. Stir in cream, bring to the boil, then reduce heat and simmer for 3-4 minutes or until mixtures reduces and thickens slightly. Stir in tomatoes, basil, chilli and black pepper to taste and, stirring constantly, bring back to the boil.

2   Add mussels to pan and cook for 5 minutes or until shells open. Discard any mussels that do not open after 5 minutes cooking. Using a slotted spoon, transfer mussels to serving bowls, then spoon over sauce.

Serves 6

Honeyed Squid Salad,
Mussels in Chilli Cream Sauce

Plate Villeroy & Boch

Above: Chicken with Lime and Tarragon
Right: Fish Cutlets with Salsa

CHICKEN WITH LIME AND TARRAGON

**8 chicken thigh fillets or 4 boneless
chicken breast fillets**
$^1/_4$ cup/30 g/1 oz seasoned flour
2 tablespoons olive oil
1 cup/250 mL/8 fl oz chicken stock
2 tablespoons lime juice
**1 tablespoon fresh tarragon or
1 teaspoon dried tarragon**
1 clove garlic, crushed
freshly ground black pepper
$^1/_2$ cup/125 mL/4 fl oz cream (double)
2 teaspoons Dijon mustard

Serve with noodles and
salad or new potatoes and
steamed or stir-fried
vegetables. If preferred,
purchase a chicken and cut
it into serving pieces – this is
usually more economical
than purchasing mixed
pieces.

1 Place chicken and seasoned flour in
a plastic food bag and toss to coat
chicken with flour. Shake off excess
flour and set aside. Heat oil in a frying
pan over a medium heat, add chicken

and cook for 3-4 minutes each side or
until brown. Remove chicken from pan
and set aside.

2 Stir stock, lime juice, tarragon,
garlic and black pepper to taste into
pan and bring to the boil, stirring to
loosen sediment. Return chicken to
pan and simmer for 20 minutes or until
chicken is tender.

3 Using a slotted spoon, remove
chicken from pan, set aside and keep
warm. Stir cream and mustard into
pan, bring to the boil and boil, stirring
constantly, until sauce reduces and
thickens. Spoon sauce over chicken
and serve.

Serves 4

FISH CUTLETS WITH SALSA

4 x 155 g/5 oz fish cutlets or
thick fillets of your choice
60 g/2 oz butter, softened
1 clove garlic, crushed
2 teaspoons finely grated lemon rind
$^{1}/_{2}$ cup/125 mL/4 fl oz dry white wine

TOMATO CUCUMBER SALSA
2 tomatoes, diced
1 onion, diced
1 small cucumber, diced
2 teaspoons chopped fresh dill
$^{1}/_{4}$ teaspoon chopped fresh red chilli
2 tablespoons lemon juice
freshly ground black pepper

1   Place fish in a shallow ovenproof dish and set aside. Place butter, garlic and lemon rind in a bowl and beat to combine. Spread butter mixture on each cutlet. Pour over wine, cover dish with foil and bake for 10-15 minutes or until fish flakes easily when tested with a fork.

2   To make salsa, combine tomatoes, onion, cucumber, dill, chilli, lemon juice and black pepper to taste in a bowl and toss. Serve with fish.

Serves 4

Oven temperature
200°C, 400°F, Gas 6

Any good value cutlets or thick boneless fish fillets can be used for this recipe. For extra spice, add a little chilli sauce to the salsa.

FRUIT FLAN

If preferred, use a ready-made pastry case, available from supermarkets. Fresh, frozen or canned fruit may be used as best buys become available.

SHORTCRUST PASTRY
1 cup/125 g/4 oz flour
60 g/2 oz butter, chopped
1 tablespoon caster sugar
1 egg yolk
1-2 tablespoons lemon juice or water

CUSTARD FILLING
2 egg yolks
1 egg
^{1}/4 cup/60 g/2 oz caster sugar
1 tablespoon flour
1 tablespoon cornflour
1^1/4 cups/315 mL/10 fl oz milk
1 teaspoon vanilla essence

FRUIT TOPPING
440 g/14 oz canned fruit of choice, drained
^{1}/4 cup/75 g/2^1/2 oz apricot conserve, warmed

1 To make pastry, sift flour into a bowl. Rub in butter with fingertips until mixture resembles coarse breadcrumbs, then stir in sugar. Add egg yolk and enough lemon juice or water to make a pliable dough. Wrap dough in plastic food wrap and refrigerate for 30 minutes.

2 Roll out pastry to 5 mm/^{1}/4 in thick and use to line a lightly greased 23 cm/9 in flan tin. Line pastry case with nonstick baking paper, fill with uncooked rice and bake for 15 minutes. Remove rice and paper and bake for 15 minutes longer or until pastry is golden. Set aside to cool.

3 To make filling, place egg yolks, egg and sugar in a bowl. Place flour and cornflour in a small bowl and blend in ^{1}/2 cup/125 mL/4 fl oz of the milk to make a smooth paste. Stir into egg mixture.

4 Place remaining milk in a saucepan and bring to the boil over a medium heat. Blend a little of the hot milk into egg mixture, then stir egg mixture into remaining milk in the saucepan. Return pan to a heat and cook over a medium heat, stirring constantly, for 4-5 minutes or until mixture boils and thickens. Reduce heat and simmer for 3 minutes. Remove pan from heat and stir in vanilla essence. Cover surface of custard with plastic food wrap and set aside to cool.

5 Spread custard over base of pastry case. Arrange fruit over custard and brush with apricot conserve to glaze.

Serves 6

Fruit Flan

Plate Waterford Wedgwood

Cassata Log

CASSATA LOG

$^1/_2$ cup/100 g/3$^1/_2$ oz caster sugar
2 tablespoons water
315 g/10 oz ricotta cheese, drained
90 g/3 oz dark chocolate, chopped
45 g/1$^1/_2$ oz mixed glacé cherries
2 tablespoons chopped candied mixed peel
2 tablespoons crushed nuts
2 tablespoons sweet sherry
1$^1/_2$ cups/375 mL/12 fl oz cream (double), whipped

1 Place sugar and water in a saucepan and bring to the boil over a medium heat, stirring until sugar dissolves. Reduce heat and simmer, without stirring, for 2 minutes. Remove pan from heat and set aside to cool slightly.

2 Push ricotta cheese through a fine sieve into a large bowl. Slowly stir sugar syrup into cheese, mixing well to combine. Add chocolate, cherries, mixed peel, nuts and sherry and mix to combine. Fold in cream.

3 Spoon mixture into a foil-lined 11 x 21 cm/4$^1/_2$ x 8$^1/_2$ in loaf tin. Cover with foil and freeze overnight. To serve, unmould and cut into slices.

Serves 6

Delicious served with thick cream and savoiardi biscuits (sponge fingers) or topped with purchased chocolate topping.

TUSCAN POTATOES

Oven temperature
200°C, 400°F, Gas 6

Your favourite dried herbs
and chopped fresh chilli
make a tasty addition to
this easy potato dish. For
yet another variation
sprinkle the potatoes with
grated Parmesan cheese
during the last 15 minutes of
cooking.

¹/₃ cup/90 mL/3 fl oz olive oil
750 g/1¹/₂ lb potatoes, scrubbed and
cut into chunks
3 cloves garlic, crushed
freshly ground black pepper

1   Place oil in a baking dish and heat
in oven for 3 minutes or until hot.

2   Add potatoes and garlic to pan and
toss to coat with oil. Sprinkle with
black pepper to taste and bake, turning
every 15 minutes, for 1 hour or until
potatoes are tender, crisp and golden.

Serves 6

SPINACH BURGHUL SALAD

Oven temperature
180°C, 350°F, Gas 4

This salad may be made
and dressed in advance –
the spinach will not be
affected by the dressing.
Sprinkle with croûtons
before serving.

2 slices bread, crusts removed, cubed
¹/₄ cup/45 g/1¹/₂ oz cracked wheat
(burghul)
¹/₄ cup/60 mL/2 fl oz water
2 tablespoons lemon juice
1 bunch/500 g/1 lb English spinach
2 tomatoes, chopped
1 onion, sliced
3 rashers bacon, grilled and chopped
2 tablespoons olive oil
1 tablespoon cider vinegar
¹/₂ teaspoon dried basil leaves

1   Place bread on a baking tray and
bake for 10 minutes or until crisp and
golden. Set aside to cool, then store in
an airtight container until needed.

2   Place cracked wheat (burghul) in
a bowl, add water and lemon juice and
mix to combine. Set aside to soak for
15 minutes or until all the liquid is
absorbed.

3   Place spinach leaves in a salad bowl,
add cracked wheat (burghul), tomatoes,
onion, bacon, oil, vinegar and basil and
toss to combine. Just prior to serving,
scatter with croûtons.

Serves 6

Spinach Burghul Salad, Tuscan Potatoes

CHEESE AND SAGE DAMPER

Oven temperature
220°C, 425°F, Gas 7

2 cups/250 g/8 oz self-raising flour
30 g/1 oz butter
60 g/2 oz grated tasty cheese
(mature Cheddar)
1 teaspoon dried sage
¹/₂ cup/125 mL/4 fl oz milk
¹/₂ cup/125 mL/4 fl oz water
sesame seeds (optional)

Try making this damper with other fresh or dried herbs in place of the sage. The key to success with damper is not to over-handle the dough, so keep the mixing and kneading to a minimum.

1   Sift flour into a bowl. Rub in butter with fingertips until mixture resembles coarse breadcrumbs. Stir in cheese and sage. Make a well in the centre of the flour mixture. Reserve 2 teaspoons of the milk. Add remaining milk and water to flour mixture and mix quickly to make a soft dough.

2   Turn mixture onto a lightly floured surface, knead lightly and divide into 6 equal pieces. Shape dough pieces into rounds and place, close together, on a greased baking tray to form a round loaf. Brush with reserved milk and sprinkle with sesame seeds, if using.

3   Bake for 15 minutes, reduce oven temperature to 190°C/375°F/Gas 5 and bake for 10-15 minutes longer or until loaf sounds hollow when tapped on the base. Serve warm.

Serves 6

INDEX

ACKNOWLEDGMENTS

The publishers thanks the following companies who generously supplied props for this book.

Royal Worcester
Available from major
department stores and gift
suppliers
Ph: (02) 498 6233

Villeroy & Boch
Available from major
department stores and gift
suppliers
Ph: (02) 975 3099
enquiries only

Waterford Wedgwood
Australia Limited
Available from major
department stores and
leading specialty stores
Ph: (02) 899 2877
enquiries only